SPIKES

Growth Hacking Leadership

JASON SCHENKER

Copyright © 2019 Prestige Professional Publishing, LLC
All rights reserved.

SPIKES

Growth Hacking Leadership

BY JASON SCHENKER

No part of this publication may be reproduced, copied, stored in or transmitted into a data retrieval system, or transmitted in any form, or by any means (electronic, mechanical, photocopying, recording, or any other method) without written permission of the publisher, Prestige Professional Publishing, LLC.

ISBN: 978-1-946197-07-8 *Paperback*
    978-1-946197-06-1 *Ebook*

For my mentors.

CONTENTS

PREFACE — 9

INTRODUCTION — 13

THE FOUNDATION OF SPIKES

CHAPTER 1
WHY I WROTE THIS BOOK — 25

CHAPTER 2
METACOGNITION — 33

CHAPTER 3
EXPERIENCE — 43

CHAPTER 4
PROJECTION — 49

CHAPTER 5
SUPPORT — 55

FOCUSING YOUR SPIKES

CHAPTER 6
FIND YOUR SPIKES — 61

CHAPTER 7
PLAN YOUR SPIKES — 69

SCALE YOUR SPIKES

CHAPTER 8
COMMIT TO YOUR SPIKES — 75

CHAPTER 9
BUILD, FEED, AND GROW YOUR SPIKES — 79

CHAPTER 10
IGNORE FAKE SPIKES — 83

CHAPTER 11
OUTSOURCE AND DELEGATE TO SPIKE — 87

CONTENTS

PROJECTING YOUR SPIKES

CHAPTER 12
SHOW YOUR SPIKES   93

CHAPTER 13
FAKE YOUR SPIKES   95

CHAPTER 14
SPIKES IN THE AUTOMATION AGE   99

FINDING THE RIGHT SUPPORT

CHAPTER 15
ENLIST SUPPORT TO BUILD SPIKES   107

CHAPTER 16
FINDING THE RIGHT SPIKE MENTOR   111

ADAPTING YOUR SPIKES

CHAPTER 17
SPIKES ON SPIKES   119

CHAPTER 18
RECYCLE YOUR SPIKES   123

CHAPTER 19
CHANGE YOUR SPIKES   127

CHAPTER 20
INVESTING IN SPIKES   131

CHAPTER 21
SPIKES AND THE ENTREPRENEUR   135

PULLING EVERYTHING TOGETHER

CHAPTER 22
HACK YOUR SPIKES   141

CONTENTS

CHAPTER 23
  SHARE YOUR SPIKES   **145**

CONCLUSION   **149**

ENDNOTES   **153**

ABOUT THE AUTHOR   **155**
RANKINGS   **159**
ABOUT THE PUBLISHER   **163**
DISCLAIMERS   **173**

PREFACE

LEADERSHIP AND SUPPORT

This is a book about leadership. But it is also a book about having support and mentorship. So it is fitting that I begin this book by acknowledging those individuals who have helped me in my career as well as those who helped make this book a reality.

I have a countless list of mentors who have helped me along the way. It became very apparent to me as I was writing this book just how many people have influenced me over the years.

Of course, there are my parents. Honestly, if you are lucky enough to have chosen your parents well, then you are off to a big head start. But beyond your family and the role models that may exist therein, there are also teachers of various kinds — those in classrooms, those in meeting rooms, and those in boardrooms.

Having spent almost as much time after high school in a classroom as outside of one, the list of teachers and professors I need to thank is quite long. And then there are my professional mentors as well.

I had teacher mentors in the fields of history, German, and economics. And I am grateful to all of them.

In the field of history, **John Heineman** of Boston College and **Martin Havran** of the University of Virginia provided me with sound guidance. Both have since passed away. In the field of German, the late **Jonathan Hess** was a valued mentor and my graduate advisor. May his memory be a blessing.

In the field of economics, I was lucky to have **Robin Watson** as a mentor. I was extremely fortunate he was on loan to the University of North Carolina at Chapel Hill when I was studying German literature. It was a pleasure to take his course then and to remain in contact with him over the years. And it pleased me greatly to be able to collaborate with him over the past year.

There have been other academic mentors along the way, including my undergraduate dean at the University of Virginia, **Frank Papovich**. And of course there have been many professional mentors.

In my career, I was lucky to work for and with a few admirable mentors: **John Schmonsees** at the U.S. Commerce Department, **John Silvia** and **Jay Bryson** at Wachovia, and **Jon Ruggles** at McKinsey. But that was years ago.

I am now 42. It's not a particularly important or significant age. But after having been an entrepreneur for a decade, there are fewer mentors around. And I realize that I have learned a few things. There are lessons worth sharing that may help others.

And that's what *Spikes: Growth Hacking Leadership* is about.

This book represents an attempt to give back, to share what I have learned along the way, to be a mentor to others so they too can develop spikes and be successful.

Beyond the mentors I need to thank, I also want to acknowledge and thank all the people who helped make this book come together. I want to especially thank **Nawfal Patel,** who managed the production of *Spikes*. I also want to thank **Kerry Ellis**, our cover designer, for bringing my ideas for the cover of this book to life. And I want to thank **Ryan Holiday** for encouraging me to write a book that goes beyond economics and technology — to write something with an evergreen message.

Most importantly, I want to thank my family for supporting me in my education, career, entrepreneurship, and authorship. I am always most grateful for the support of my loving wife, **Ashley Schenker**, and to my wonderful parents, **Janet and Jeffery Schenker**. My family supports me in countless ways by providing emotional support and editorial feedback.

Every time I write a book, it's a crazy experience that spills over into my family life, so to them and to everyone else who helped me in this process: Thank you!

Finally, thank you for buying this book. I hope you enjoy *Spikes: Growth Hacking Leadership*!

~ Jason Schenker

INTRODUCTION

SPIKES: AN INTRODUCTION

What makes a leader?

In most cases, leadership takes experience, education, and skill.

It also takes a person with the *savoir faire* to get promoted, start a successful business, or fund a profitable business. But while most leadership takes years to achieve, there is a way to shorten the process.

Spikes.

There is a set process of success. And like all processes, it can be hacked. This doesn't mean you are writing computer code. We aren't talking about that kind of hacking.

Growth hacking is when you figure out the secret to making rapid progress to achieve growth. In this case, it means cracking the secret code to grow as a leader — to achieve leadership rapidly.

Spikes are Everything

Simply defined, spikes are areas of expertise.

You may never have heard about spikes before, but they are an open secret in the consulting world.

When I worked at McKinsey and Company, a firm that is widely regarded as one of the top management consulting firms in the world, people talked about spikes. If you showed skills, knowledge, and abilities that were above average, people referred to these as spikes.

To be successful, you needed to have spikes in multiple areas. But there is a balance between having too few and too many spikes.

Striking that balance is as important in consulting as it is in all industries.

Spikes are Distinctive

Another way consultants speak about spikes is to call these kinds of attributes "distinctive."

These spikes — these distinctive attributes — are important for success in consulting, whether you are at McKinsey, Booz Allen, Accenture, or Deloitte.

In fact, it's difficult to get hired into consulting without demonstrating expertise — without showing that you have spikes or at least the making of future spikes.

While distinctive spikes are critical for success in consulting, they are also essential to succeeding at any business endeavor. Whether you work in a large public corporation, a private company, a consulting firm, a startup, an NGO, or in the government, spikes are necessary ingredients to getting ahead.

The good news is that you don't have to be good at everything. You just have to be good at a couple of things. But the better you are at things, the more spikey you will be.

And the bigger your spikes, the more professional impact you can have.

The purpose of this book is to help you on your quest to find your spikes, build your spikes, and shorten your time to successful leadership.

Spikes are the way you hack your way to rapidly growing into a leadership position. And you can augment your own innate abilities with the help of others.

Spikes will catapult you to success. They'll make you stand out, and they will stick anyone who gets in your way.

This book will help you get those spikes, hack your way to leadership, and catapult your career to success.

Together, we will be growth hacking leadership.

The Spikes Formula

Perhaps it's because I worked in finance or maybe because I worked in consulting that I think it is important to codify the concept of spikes and leadership as a formula:

Spikes = f {Metacognition, Experience, Projection, Support}

As you can see, in the framework I created as part of The Futurist Institute's training program, there are four elements of having spikes — of being a leader and an expert.

These include metacognition, experience, projection, and support. I will discuss each of these at length later in this book, but let's do a quick overview of these concepts.

Metacognition — This is the ability to learn new things and to know how you learn so that you can become an expert rapidly. This is a critical part of hacking the leadership game. But it's a skill that takes decades to really hone. The good news is that you've been learning new things since the day you were born!

Experience — Obviously, to be seen as an expert and a leader, you have to have experience. Unfortunately, many people think this is the only element that matters to being a leader. Some think that it's just a numbers game and you need to just check off the years until you are recognized. But that isn't true.

Some people have a ton of experience but are not viewed as thought leaders. Meanwhile, some people may have relatively little experience in terms of years but be viewed as experts.

This is because experience is only one part of having spikes.

This is because the amount of experience you have is not just a time-bound element of leadership success. The type of experience, your effort, and the other elements that help you build your spikes can make this one of the areas with flexible time commitments. This doesn't mean that you can skirt by and become an expert without doing real work and without gaining real experience.

But it does mean that leveraging the other elements of spikes — metacognition, projection, and support — can reduce the actual amount of time you need to be grinding away to prove you are an expert. And time is your most valuable and most limited resource.

Projection — This is one of the biggest parts of leverage for building spikes. While learning new things rapidly due to high metacognition capabilities can help you develop expertise rapidly, only projection can shape the views of the external world into seeing you as an expert and a leader.

If you are expert and no one knows it, are you really an expert?

You may be. But you aren't a trusted thought leader in the broader sense of the word. We will revisit this topic later in the book, and I will share some critical tricks and tips to projecting your expertise and knowledge in a way to craft your image as a thought leader that will lead to promotions, consulting gigs, and other opportunities for you to get paid to share your wisdom.

Support — This is the fourth and final important ingredient to developing spikes and being seen as a thought leader. In short, we all go through life only once. But by leveraging the experiences of others — by having strong mentors and trusted advisors and by building a personal board of directors — can you accelerate the learning process to navigate unforeseen challenges ahead.

In tandem with metacognition, support provides a shortcut to the big challenges that can stall out your leadership development.

Growth Hacking Leadership
If you can tackle the spikes equation and lever metacognition, experience, projection, and support, you will be on your way to being a recognized expert — to being a thought leader.

And that is the goal of this book: to guide you through that process. It is a support element designed to help you succeed.

The Structure of This Book
In order to tackle the most important factors in navigating *Spikes: Growth Hacking Leadership*, I have divided this book into seven sections:
- **The Foundation of Spikes**
- **Focusing Your Spikes**
- **Scale Your Spikes**
- **Projecting Your Spikes**
- **Finding the Right Support**
- **Adapting Your Spikes**
- **Pulling Everything Together**

In the first section of *Spikes: Growth Hacking Leadership*, **The Foundation of Spikes**, I discuss the four elements of building spikes in detail — and I share how these elements have worked for me and how they can work for you! I discuss why I wrote this book and the importance of spikes in Chapter 1. In Chapter 2, I discuss the importance of metacognition for building spikes, especially as it relates to the value of formal education and having a learning process. In Chapter 3, I discuss the importance and value of work experience. And it's not just about checking off years while you mark time. The significance of your experience is critical, and I discuss why this is so important. In Chapter 4, I discuss the value of projection in detail. There are two major elements you need to consider around projecting expertise and thought leadership: internal and external perception. The final chapter in this section of the book is Chapter 5, in which I discuss the importance of support elements for building sound spikes. In general, the first section of this book lays the groundwork for the approaches you will take to the spikes that you choose to adopt. And this is a main part of the second section of the book.

In the second section, **Focusing Your Spikes**, I discuss some of the most important best practices when selecting the spikes you want to build up — and how to focus your efforts and avoid distractions to maximize your potential satisfaction, success, and reputation as a thought leader. In Chapter 6, I discuss how to look for and find your potential spikes. Then, in Chapter 7, I discuss how to plan your spikes — and the importance of managing one field of expertise at a time. After all, you don't want to end up a jack of all trades and master of none. You can be a master of many things, but it starts with one.

The third section of this book is dedicated to **Scale Your Spikes**. In Chapter 8, I discuss committing to your spikes and how building expertise is like investing in a startup — start small, then scale. Then, in Chapter 9, I discuss some of the best ways to build, feed, and grow your spikes. In Chapter 10, I offer some advice on ignoring fake spikes. Remaining focused is key, but there are often distractions. You need to avoid these as much as possible.

In Chapter 11, I discuss the importance of outsourcing things that are not spikes either through delegation or automation. This is another way to drown out the noise of fake spikes — and to allow for significant focus on what you do best and where you want to be a thought leader.

The fourth section of *Spikes: Growth Hacking Leadership* is titled **Projecting Your Spikes**. In Chapter 12, I discuss how you can show your spikes, and I discuss the various ways you can project your expertise and thought leadership. In this section, I also make the almost-radical assertion that you might need to fake your spikes in Chapter 13. This doesn't mean you are a fraud or doing anything illegal. But it does mean that you may suffer from imposter syndrome and that for a time you might need to "fake it till you make it."

In Chapter 14, I discuss spikes in the automation age and discuss some explicit examples of how you can use technology to advance your projection. And how you can maximize the effectiveness of projecting your spikes.

In the fifth section of this book, **Finding the Right Support**, I discuss the places to look for support. In Chapter 15, this includes different professional and personal contacts that can help you in your quest to become a thought leader. In Chapter 16, I discuss more explicitly the importance of having a professional mentor who has already been down the professional path you are treading.

In this book's sixth section, **Adapting Your Spikes**, the focus is on adapting and replicating spikes in order to build out a broader and more comprehensive thought-leadership platform. In Chapter 17, I discuss how to build spikes on spikes and leverage the spikes you already have to build new ones. Then, in Chapter 18, I discuss how to recycle your spikes and be more efficient. In Chapter 19, I discuss how to change your spikes, and the focus of Chapter 20 is thinking about spikes as an investment. In the last part of this section — in Chapter 21 — I discuss the entrepreneurial nature of building spikes — and also how entrepreneurs need to think of spikes.

In this book's seventh and final section, **Pulling Everything Together**, I tie in themes shared throughout this book in order to present some important actionable recommendations. This book is about having a comprehensive strategy to hack the process of building spikes to become a recognized leader. And Chapter 22 brings it all together. But that isn't the way the book ends. I end the book with a call to action in Chapter 23, in which I encourage you to share your spikes — to help others build and hack their own way to leadership.

The Foundation of Spikes

CHAPTER 1

WHY I WROTE THIS BOOK

It takes a lot of work to become a leader.

Since experience is a critical element to becoming a leader, it can take a lot of time to achieve a leadership role.

And time is your most valuable asset. Your rarest and least renewable commodity.

This is why I wrote this book.

There are only two ways to gain experience: learn for yourself or aggregate the experience of others to leapfrog a process that can be long, tedious, difficult, and boring.

But there is an easier way.

I wanted to share my experiences in leadership and business to help you save time. To help you learn from my mistakes — and to learn from the leadership example of others. And all of those examples draw from the same assets: spikes.

This Book is for Aspiring Leaders
This book isn't for everyone.

- If you are content being one of the masses, this book isn't for you.
- If you are happy slaving away and being at the bottom of the pecking order in a large corporation, this book isn't for you.
- If you are content to take your time to find a leadership role, this book isn't for you.

But, if you want to hack a system that tells you that you have to wait your turn to be a leader, this is the book for you.

You don't need to wait. You can begin your path to leadership now. All you need are spikes.

And we can cut short your search for them.

That is the big idea of this book. To help you become a leader quickly — to help you hack the system.

My Experience
I was never happy when people told me I had to wait to be a leader. I never liked the idea of waiting my turn to be the boss. I didn't want to wait. And you shouldn't have to wait either.

I used the resources I had — the ability to learn rapidly and a strong network — to build or start a successful career. Then I used my experience and ability to project that expertise to found multiple successful businesses.

Of course, everyone's situation is different. But my ability to learn new things and my network helped me at every stage of my professional development.

And those are two of the core elements of the formula for spikes:

Spikes = f {Metacognition, Experience, Projection, Support}

It turns out that I stumbled into these two valuable elements of having spikes almost entirely by accident. Yet metacognition and support helped me start my career.

My very first "real job" was at one of the biggest investment banks in the United States. In my role as an economist, I made some bold and accurate predictions about oil prices in 2004. I was subsequently recognized as the bank's Chief Energy Economist. This means that I was giving important keynote speeches and doing interviews on CNBC television and Bloomberg television in less than a year.

So how did I get that job? I got it by tapping my network and projecting potential. In the absence of expertise, it was all I had.

At that time, I was almost 27 and had found a number of strong mentors, but I had not yet had a real career job. But I leveraged what I had. I reached out to my most serious mentors. They wrote me letters of recommendation, they vouched for me, and in the absence of significant professional experience, they helped me project the potential for spikes. In that moment, more than perhaps any other, my network — my support — helped me.

It's generally a good spike to have, and it happens to be one of my strongest — even now. In the end, I got the job because of my network support and my ability to project expertise and ability.

But how did I get good at that job? I leveraged another key element of spikes: my ability to learn — that metacognition piece. In short, I got good at the job by learning things quickly.

I even picked up another core element while in banking: experience. And it was enough experience to demonstrate spikes in commodities, currencies, and economics. A lot of that ability to project was based on the nature of the role, where I was doing daily television, radio, and print media hits.

When I saw the financial crisis coming, I leaned on my experience, my ability to project expertise, my network, and my ability to learn rapidly to land my next role at McKinsey and Company. And I even landed a role as a Risk Specialist, where I was recognized for having specialized expertise.

I had developed a true spike as a thought leader in commodities and financial markets in under four years by leveraging the four key elements of spikes: metacognition, experience, projection, and support.

And things only accelerated from there, allowing me to start my own firm less than two years later. After stints in banking and consulting, I started Prestige Economics in 2009. And I have continued to build and establish new professional spikes.

Some of this has to do with projection. After all, Bloomberg News has recognized me as one of the top forecasters in the world for the accuracy of my economic and financial market forecasts as the President of Prestige Economics.

My track record between 2011 and the fourth quarter of 2018 has included top rankings for my forecast accuracy across 43 different categories, including accuracy rankings as #1 in the world in 25 different categories. Simply put, there is no other financial market futurist in world with this level of accuracy in predicting the future.

Most people never get to say they are #1 in the world at anything. They never get to have spikes like that. But it happens to me every quarter.

You see, every quarter, I receive rankings for the work I do, and I use my spikes to be the best.

The rankings come because of my experience and skill at what I do. But the ability to project those rankings is extremely valuable.

More recently, I have become involved in building up The Futurist Institute to help people build spikes in understanding the strategic implications of future technology. Of course, in order to help others, I had to build spikes in this area first. And that took time.

But it took even less time to build my spikes as a futurist than it did to build my spikes in financial markets.

And that's why I wanted to share this story.

Because I can see that every time you build spikes, it gets easier — and it comes more quickly. In fact, even now, I am sure that my next spikes will come even more quickly.

I used to think my story was not unique. But I recently began to realize that it is. Some people spend their whole career building just one spike.

And for some that may be enough.

But not for me.

And it shouldn't be for you either!

Your Spikes
I believe that everyone has the ability to be the best in the world at something — at multiple things. All it takes are the right elements in the spikes equation.

Of course, each individual situation is different, and it would be easier to build spikes for some in certain areas rather than others. But once that part is narrowed down, the upside potential is massive.

You have to find your own spikes, you have to feed those spikes, and sometimes you even have to fake those spikes in order to make a rapid jump to a leadership role or to become an established thought leader.

I have to admit that I am humbly and continually surprised by my spikes.

And if you muster the core elements of spikes, you may be surprised by your own success — and by how rapidly you achieve a leadership role. Whether you've been building up your expertise in different areas for years, or if you are just now trying to find a way to break out, this book will help you get there.

I have spikes — and you do too!

Now, let's get you there!

CHAPTER 2

METACOGNITION

The first of the four parts of building spikes to become a leader is metacognition. Simply put, this is learning how to learn.

Some of us are quicker learners than others.

I am pretty sure that I was the only kid in the world who knew their Social Security number in the fourth grade. And that's probably what you might expect from the son of an accountant. And someone writing a leadership book that is rooted in a formula.

But almost no one is instantly a good learner at everything.

In fact, I almost failed kindergarten because I couldn't tie my shoelaces. Eventually, I muddled through with the whole "two bunny ears" shortcut. And I only learned how to properly tie my shoelaces when I was getting ready to graduate from college.

The early part of life isn't necessarily just about learning little facts or gaining rudimentary capabilities, like a first-level video game player trying to level up. The truth is that the most important thing we learn as children, in our secondary education and well through college — if we are lucky enough to have the proper guidance — is how to learn.

Although this process was assumed to be adopted and learned almost by osmosis for most of human history, it has gained more recent traction as a concept known as metacognition.

Metacognition is thinking about how you learn — not about learning itself.

That means that metacognition isn't about being good at things instantly. Nor is metacognition about learning things that come easily — or learning things that are more difficult.

The theory was created and first espoused in 1979 by John Flavell, who is viewed as a founding scholar of the field. In fact, the truth is that you may be able to learn more about how to learn from the things that are more difficult and challenging.

In short, it's an active and strategic process of learning how to learn.

It's how individuals at a strategic and almost detached level have thoughts about learning. That's the *meta* part of metacognition. It is the self-assessed and self-observed process that is developed while learning.

As defined by the education company Actively Learn:

> Metacognition is an awareness of one's own learning. It entails understanding the goals of the learning process, figuring out the best strategies for learning, and assessing whether the learning goals are being met. A metacognitive student sees him or herself as an agent in the learning process and realizes that learning is an active, strategic activity.[1]

In other words, more advanced students, if they are metacognitive, think strategically about what they are trying to learn. And this is a skill that can carry forward into professional careers. In fac, this is a critical ingredient, not just an optional skill.

The ability to learn strategically and rapidly is a critical element for education and professional success — and for building a platform to have spikes and project yourself as a leader.

And this is one of the things that students are expected to absorb as part of their education that they find disinteresting.

Put simply, there are things you don't want to learn in life, but the process of learning those things helps prepare you for a life in which you will inevitably have to learn many things you don't want to have to learn. And this is just as true for the general education college courses you may not like as it is for that office job where you have to learn how to navigate a computer program or software interface that you find unpleasant or annoying.

In fact, the more recently maligned and askantly viewed traditional argument in favor of liberal arts education has been organically and rather unsystematically built around this notion.

And the value and notion that learning to learn complex concepts and new things that are unfamiliar — and even things you do not like — presents a value later in life when you actually have to do the same thing out in the real world.

An active metacognitive approach includes three parts: a learning process, the task of learning, and strategies to get there.[2]

Actively Learn more broadly articulates a number of important elements of metacognition that could include the following:

- *Understanding what one already knows about a topic.*
- *Figuring out what one wants to know about a topic.*
- *Realizing what one has learned in the course of a lesson.*
- *Monitoring one's understanding during the course of an activity.*
- *Choosing which learning strategies to employ and when.*
- *Evaluating whether a particular learning strategy was successful in a given circumstance.*[3]

Although the discussion around metacognition is often framed in terms of courses and schooling, the truth is that in all professional endeavors you are required to learn new things.

It is the speed with which you can get up the learning curve that is critical.

This is why the three elements of a learning process, the task of learning, and the strategies to get there are still the same.

Applying a Metacognitive Professional Framework
Now that I've shared some information about metacognition, let's look at applying it to a couple of real-world scenarios.

First, let's look at learning a foreign language. Imagine you want to learn French or Spanish or German.

If we consider the structure already articulated and apply it to learning this foreign language, I argue that it might look like this:

1. **Understanding what you know.**
- What do you know about the foreign language you want to learn?
- Do you know some words, some grammar, or context?
- Do you know a language with similar words?
- Do you have exposure to a language with similar grammar?

2. **Figuring out what you want to know.**
- What capabilities do you want to have in the target language?
- How quickly do you want to reach the target fluency?
- How good do you want your accent to be?
- Do you need to actively use the language, or are passive skills sufficient?

3. **Realizing what you learned.**
- Have you learned the actual words needed to communicate?
- Do you have an understanding of the grammar?

4. **Monitoring your understanding.**
   - Are you retaining information?
   - Are you able to integrate new learnings?
   - Are you tracking to your goals and target competencies?
   - How are you testing your knowledge?

5. **Choosing learning strategies to employ.**
   - Will you immerse yourself in the language?
   - Will you practice and absorb key words and phrases using rote memorization?
   - How will you practice your language skills to make them interactive?
   - How will you build your passive knowledge?

6. **Evaluating the success of a learning strategy.**
   - Was the process as effective as you expected?
   - Did you keep to your intended timeline?
   - Were you able to perform the tasks you wanted to?
   - Did you reach your target fluency?

Now, let's consider a more professionally-oriented concept.

Perhaps the language you want — or rather need — to learn is not French or Spanish or German as you may have imagined.

Imagine that the language is SAS or Stata or another computer programming language, like Python. Now, you are applying a metacognitive framework to a new learning process. A process with a potentially important professional impact and a likely financial ROI.

Following this same structure of planning could arguably help you get up that learning curve faster. It could shorten the time it takes you to learn. And it could open up new professional opportunities. It could help you become a leader and build a spike.

And this example isn't just a story. It's my story.

I learned French for seven years before beginning to learn German. And I learned German much more quickly because I followed this kind of process. In fact, the time from my first German course to the time I was accepted into a German PhD program with full funding was only about 30 months.

But the story didn't end there.

After I finished my graduate degree in German literature, I began a master's in applied economics. And a major focus of that degree was on using software to do statistical analyses. This included computer programming languages like SAS and Stata.

This is exactly the kind of challenge where previous academic learning processes could be applied to accelerate learning something professionally-oriented as part of a process of learning something different yet similar. And as you can see, translating your ability to learn across fields and across tasks isn't just something that exists as subtext or as theory.

Even at the time I made my own transition to learning statistical computer programming languages, this was explicitly addressed.

When the department chair of economics offered me a slot in the graduate program for applied economics, he even said to me that computer programs were just another kind of language. And he noted his optimism about my potential for success after having learned about my ability to learn other languages.

This allusion to learning how to learn — to metacognition — was clear, even though the word *metacognition* never came up.

Using Metacognative Arguments to Overcome a Catch-22
Throughout your career, you will also be forced to make professional changes and leaps. Tying into your past experience to succeed at future challenges will be critical for your success.

Chances are, you may have already done this in your academic and professional career without even thinking about it. You may have been applying your metacognitive abilities as second nature, without even thinking about it.

But now that you know about metacognition, I hope that this helps accelerate your academic and professional learning to an even greater degree. And it can help you to get a new job just as it can help to advance your career, adapt to new professional responsibilities, and foster your development as a thought leader.

When thinking about a new job, applying metacognitive concepts can help you overcome the two-part Catch-22 that is as old as time:
- How do you get a job without experience?
- But how do you get experience without a job?

As in my own story, the only want to overcome this insurmountable challenge is to find a way to make past experiences support your next challenges ahead. You have to tie things together.

Of course, once you have that new job or those new responsibilities, you will need to rely further on delivering on the assertion that what is new is old. That your new tasks ahead are similar to those behind you. If you want to build spikes — if you want to be a leader — you have to hack this challenge. And metacognition is the only way to get there.

Strategic Planning

There are many resources in terms of formal and informal education. Formal, structured education is one of the greatest ways to be forced into a process of learning how to learn. And this is especially true at the collegiate level. But whether formal or informal, the more new things you have access to learn, the better off you will be.

I am a huge advocate of perpetual learning. But unstructured perpetual learning is not enough. It is not enough to be engaged in perpetual learning. You should be strategic about your perpetual learning. You should develop, implement, and monitor your process for learning. The more structured your learning process and the more actively you apply metacognitive structures, the more rapidly you can scale your learning. This will help you build spikes and accelerate your transition to a leadership role as well as help you adopt the mantle of a thought leader.

CHAPTER 3

EXPERIENCE

To be a leader and to have spikes, you have to have experience.

One of the oldest and most proven kinds of leadership rests most firmly on experience. On time.

But experience is only one of four levers that drive spikes — that can help you build your career as a leader — and your platform as a thought leader. And experience isn't the only element of success. In truth, it has never been the only element of success.

And perhaps most importantly, experience isn't just a calendar-bound phenomenon. Gone are the days when most people spent their entire lives at one company and worked there for decades before obtaining a leadership position.

Today, it is much more common for leaders to be recognized for what they have accomplished, rather than for how many years they have logged at a given job.

Even now, you can work in an industry for decades, but unless you are pushing yourself to learn new things in that industry, to stay ahead of trends, to dive deeply into the challenges, advances, and nuances of that industry, it will be difficult for others to see you as a leader. This is tied to the importance of projecting, which I will discuss in the next chapter. But it is also tied to doing things of significance and of not just marking time.

The jobs I held in investment banking and consulting were not just 40-hour-per-week jobs. Those were jobs that demanded closer to 80 hours per week. At the time, I knew people who thought that was crazy and a waste of time.

Some people looked at it as a company's borderline abuse of its workers. That's one perspective. And it's a perspective that horribly discounts the value that I derived from working those hours.

Consider if I had instead worked 40 hours per week for six years. Those would be the normal hours for a normal gig. I would have had six years' experience for my six years of work in consulting and banking.

But by working 80 hours per week for six years, I packed in closer to 12 years of work experience at a normal job. I was able to double the amount of experience I was gaining by putting more hours in at the office.

And in the end, I was the beneficiary.

Without that experience and without that time, I would not have been able to start my own firm. I would not have had enough experience to be seen as a thought leader.

The technology guru and CEO Elon Musk once said, "No one changes the world on 40 hours per week."[1]

Praise for Musk is often overhyped. And not everyone who works more than 40 hours per week is trying to change the world. I know I wasn't. But the point here is that if you want to have significant success, you must put in a significant effort. You must have a distinctive experience.

This is important to consider this the next time you are putting time in at your job. You aren't just giving your hours to your company. After all, you are being paid for your work.

But if you are strategic about what you are learning — and about what you are dedicating your time to at work — you can reap long-term rewards by accelerating your experience in a short period of time.

This isn't to say that the only way to get experience is with years. You can accelerate the number of years by putting in more hours in those years. And you can further accelerate the timeline by putting in high-quality work in those years.

There is almost no way to remove experience from the equation of being a leader or being recognized as a thought leader. Spikes cannot exist without foundations.

And neither can your career grow without a solid foundation.

But you don't just have to mark time. You can make the most of the years you invest. And you must always have the end in mind.

Every hour you invest in your job is an hour of experience with potential long-term rewards and professional payouts. Of course, you also need to balance your work commitments with what you can handle. If you burn out, it will be for nothing.

During one part of my career, I was working 100 hours per week. I was learning a ton. I was working a ton. I was building a skill set to start my own business. But at 100 hours per week, my body just couldn't handle it. And I ended up in a hospital with kidney stones.

So, that was not great.

But at 80 hours per week, I could manage it. And I was pleased with the outcome. Most everyone I know who worked that hard became very successful, either within their banking or consulting organizations — or elsewhere.

Many of my former colleagues were able to leverage their compressed experience in a short burst of time to hop off the proverbial crazy 80-hour workweek treadmill to both earn more money and work fewer hours. My choice was a bit different, as I used my experience to build multiple successful businesses and build a thought-leadership platform.

What you do with your significant work experience is up to you. But the important thing is that if you properly manage your experience, you can monetize it in a significant and meaningful way thereafter — and long after the 80-hour-per-week corporate job is in the rearview mirror.

Experience Outside the Office
So far, I've only discussed the value of experience in the office at your job. But that is really only one element of your progression to being seen as a leader — only one part of the professional experience and being a respected thought leader.

There are also important extracurricular professional activities that can help you build your spikes and advance your professional leadership and thought-leader status.

Even though you may be fully dedicated to your job, a lot of work advancements for your personal role as a leader and for your long-term career happen outside your actual job. They may be tied to your job and profession, but they are separate. Examples of this kind of experience include conferences, volunteer activities, and making professional connections outside your company.

Maybe you've heard the phrase "Dress for the job you want, not the job you have." In many ways, this is the purpose of aggregating work-related experiences outside work. Every conference you attend, every speech you give, and every LinkedIn connection you make is a potential move toward a more significant professional experience.

As with perpetual learning, perpetual experience is critical to becoming a leader. Very few experts stop learning after their first or second job. In order to build a significant work experience, you need to be doing more things, different things, new things. The more experiences you can amass, the greater your experience will be. It's as true with the hours per week at your desk as it is with attending conferences or being involved in external professional or leadership organizations.

These kinds of experiences also help with projecting your expertise beyond your immediate circle of colleagues. And projection is a critical element of building spikes — and of becoming a leader and establishing yourself as a thought leader.

It is also the subject of the next chapter.

CHAPTER 4

PROJECTION

The third part of building spikes and becoming a leader is projecting your experience and expertise. You may have learned a ton, you may know everything about your industry, and you may be a genius in your field.

But if no one knows, it doesn't matter.

Projecting your expertise is critical and can help you significantly augment your experience. It can also help you leverage the time you have committed and the work you have done.

In addition to the experience you get at your job and the experiences you have outside work that are directly or tangentially related to your profession, you need to project your knowledge and expertise.

Actually gaining experience is the tough part, and it requires time. Projecting your experience helps you further monetize the hard work you have already put into your career.

The most important thing to know about projection is that there are internal and external projection elements as you build spikes. Both are important for your career — and for your advancement to becoming recognized as a leader.

On the one hand, the internal projection piece is important for building your support and reputation within your company. This can impact your promotability, your compensation, and the opportunities you have to convey your expertise externally.

External Projection
External projection of experience and expertise includes speeches, books, articles, videos, podcasts, radio interviews, press articles, press releases, and television interviews.

In general, these fall into established venues, traditional media, social media, and other new media, which is a mix of social and traditional media.

The easiest of these perception platforms to use is **projection on social media**. For professional purposes, LinkedIn offers the greatest projection potential, although some people use Facebook, Twitter, or Instagram to project experience, expertise, or otherwise cultivate the perception of their experience.

The next easiest of these perception levers to obtain is **projection in new media,** by writing articles on Medium, LinkedIn, or Quora. There are no barriers to entry and, if you write something significant, other people in your field may take note.

Projection can also occur in **established venues**, such as speeches at internal company events, industry conferences, and publications of your research in magazines for your profession or trade.

Projection on traditional media is the most difficult to obtain, and it often involves the use of press-relations firms to acquire what is known in the industry as "earned media." This is the most impressive to the average person; it includes press quotes, radio interviews, and television interviews.

The final critical type of external projection that can have a significant impact on your professional development is **projection with books**. Books are a more time-consuming, significant, and comprehensive way to project your expertise.

The good news with publishing and sharing your knowledge is that there are fewer limitations than ever before. There are fewer rules, but source attribution remains a critical element of securing respect through your projection.

It is also important to consider that there is a potential for content overlap between projection platforms. This means that you can also reuse content across platforms.

Internal Projection
As with external projection, there is also an important need to convey expertise within your organization in order to advance your career.

Some of the ways you project expertise internally are likely to be similar to the ways you project expertise externally.

As with external projection, information sharing and dissemination are the most important parts of projecting expertise internally. And internal corporate projection is absolutely critical because many people's assessments of their colleagues are driven by perception. After all, in many corporate structures, people aren't there very long.

In fact, they are only likely to be there for three to four years.

To support this point, I would highlight the most recent data from the U.S. Bureau of Labor Statistics, which shows that the average tenure for a job is 4.2 years for all workers over age 16. Furthermore, for younger workers, the tenure is much shorter. For workers age 25 to 34, the average tenure is only 2.8 years.[1]

For this reason, perception of expertise becomes the de facto ersatz for actual exposure to someone's work. And the perceived expectations replace actual peer-to-peer awareness of expertise.

This dynamic is particularly pronounced in the consulting world and in project-based work environments.

For example, in the consulting world, where people may only work directly together for a few months, I have seen on more than one occasion that someone who was involved with just one project was considered an expert.

Similar dynamics can be present in project-based environments, where people may only work together for short periods of time. In such instances, perception of experience and expertise can be just as important as actual experience.

In order to accelerate your path to leadership, you need to project experience both externally and internally. The better you are at projecting your experience, the more rapidly you are likely to find yourself in increasingly important leadership positions.

CHAPTER 5

SUPPORT

The fourth critical element of building spikes and becoming a recognized leader is support.

Some people call this mentorship; others call it a network. In truth, it is a mix of both. But no matter what you call it, support is always about people. And to build a significant career and become a recognized leader, you have to rely on the experiences of others. If you can aggregate what others have learned before you, it will accelerate your own learning process and professional advancement.

When I was in graduate school, I had a stack of business drawers, and one was filled with business cards. "It's all about people" was written on the outside of the drawer. It was true then, and it's still true now.

Whether you work in a large corporation, a startup, a small business, or your own entrepreneurial endeavor, people will pave the pathway to success. It's important to remember that.

One important way that I envision support is with a personal board of directors. It's something I've thought about for a long time. And it was especially important for me in my earlier career.

In my book *Recession-Proof*, I wrote about the concept of "You Inc." That you are a company. And like any company, you need a board.

The board can have anyone on it you want, but these should be people who support you fully. It can be relatives — like your parents. Or it can include a former professor, a current colleague, a past co-worker, or even a former boss. But no matter who is on your personal board, you should surround yourself mentally with this support.

These should be people whose opinions you solicit when you are making a big change — especially a big professional change. As you make big professional moves, it's important to consult your board of directors. Especially if your brand, if your spikes, if your leadership is an extension of You Inc., this is critical.

Keep in mind that no man is his own mountain range of spikes. We all draw on the knowledge and experience of others — in our families, in our company, in our communities, and in our past. If you can leverage the support of others — and most importantly, the wisdom of others — this is one of the greatest ways to reduce the amount of time you need to be having unpleasant experiences. If you can learn from others' mistakes and successes, you will go farther.

One of the biggest challenges when it comes to mustering support, having a professional network, and finding a mentor is when you have been in school, where mentors are largely academic. Another major challenge when it comes to support and support and mentorship is if you have been out of the workforce for a number of years, and your network has gone a bit cold.

Those first entering or re-entering the workforce will struggle to use this lever to propel themselves rapidly to a leadership role. But with time these will come. You just need to get in the door. And you may look for support outside the working world.

In any case, you will find it difficult to build spikes without support. After all, no leader stands alone. So, if you want to hack the path to leadership, try and find people who can lead the way — and maybe even some who can help pull you up.

Focusing Your Spikes

CHAPTER 6

FIND YOUR SPIKES

There are many different ways to find the initial signs of potential spikes.

The three most common places to look are:
- **School**
- **Work**
- **Hobbies**

In this chapter, we will visit each of these areas as fertile hunting ground for potential spikes. They all have potential, and your future spikes may be in one — or all — of those categories.

If you're like me — and like everyone else — you are probably terrible at some things, mediocre at a lot of things, and really good at a few things.

It's in those areas where you have innate abilities that you need to build. Those are the origins of spikes.

Find Your Spikes in School

School isn't the only place you can find your spikes, but it is a good place to start looking. After all, in high school you are essentially forced to take a lot of different subjects. As with everything else in life, you were better at some than others. Even if you were the valedictorian of your class, chances are you still had a strong preference for certain subjects. You excelled.

For me, it was history. I know it sounds like a weird place to start since I'm now an executive, an investor, and a finance guy. But history was my thing.

I took the AP European History exam even though my school didn't even offer AP European History courses. I got a three, which wasn't great. But since I had never taken a class on it, I was pretty happy. It also told me something about my own spikes because I also got a three on the AP Biology exam, despite the fact that I had taken three years of high school biology.

By any stretch of the imagination, I should have done better in the subject where I had had three years of instruction, compared to the course where I had had zero classes. And that pointed me in a certain direction as I went to college. There was no doubt in my mind that I was not going to be a biologist.

My story is pretty normal. School provided me with some inclinations as to what my spikes might be. And that's the purpose of education — to know where you want to get experience.

Education can help you find spikes — and it can help you learn how to build spikes.

Few children have massive spikes from an early age. And it's difficult to know what spikes will lead to your success. It is almost impossible to know what will lead to your first spike.

But you have to be on the lookout for abilities.

Not everyone needs a lot of formal education to be successful, but it is the most proven path to building a career, to finding success, and to earning more money.

In Figure 6-1, you can see statistics on unemployment and earnings from 2018 from the U.S. Bureau of Labor Statistics. Education is positively correlated with income, and education is also inversely correlated with unemployment.

In other words, generally speaking, the more education you have, the more money you make and the lower the chance that you are unemployed.

Of course, school isn't the only requirement for spikes, but it does provide a lot of opportunities for individuals to discover more and different potential spikes. It provides the potential to build metacognitive abilities as well as the opportunity to identify potential areas of interest and eventual expertise.

The same is true for math or English or any other subject that you may not have enjoyed, and you may not have had an emerging spike in these subjects. These were subjects where other people discovered they had spikes.

I've spent most of my life in school. I've done three complete master's degrees, more than a half-dozen professional certifications, and countless other forms of formal and informal education.

I think education offers the greatest ability to explore spikes: in subject areas, in writing, in communicating, and in many other areas. Plus, some professions require very specialized and advanced education, like in the fields of medicine, law, and a number of scientific professions.

Figure 6-1: Wages and Unemployment by Education Level[1]

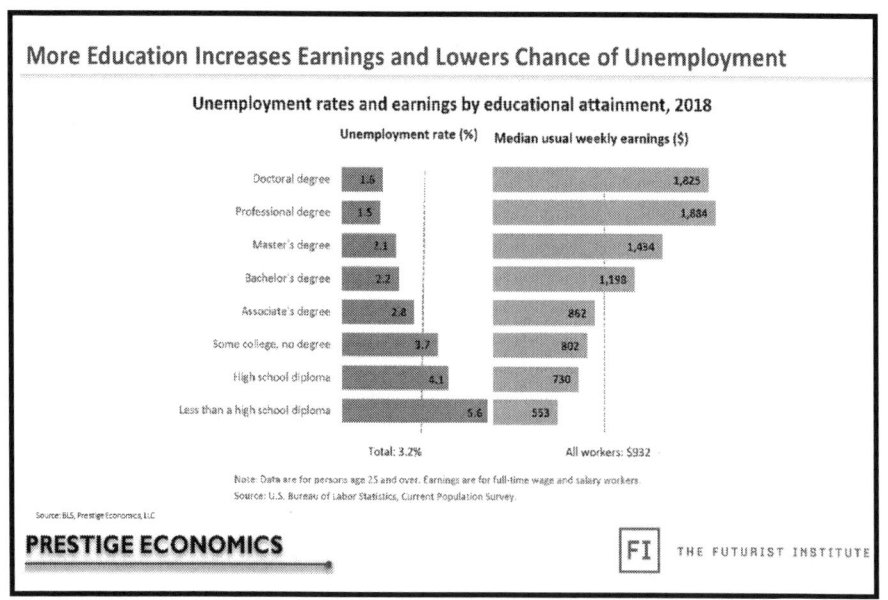

More Education Increases Earnings and Lowers Chance of Unemployment

Unemployment rates and earnings by educational attainment, 2018

Education Level	Unemployment rate (%)	Median usual weekly earnings ($)
Doctoral degree	1.6	1,825
Professional degree	1.5	1,884
Master's degree	2.1	1,434
Bachelor's degree	2.2	1,198
Associate's degree	2.8	862
Some college, no degree	3.7	802
High school diploma	4.1	730
Less than a high school diploma	5.6	553

Total: 3.2%   All workers: $932

Note: Data are for persons age 25 and over. Earnings are for full-time wage and salary workers.
Source: U.S. Bureau of Labor Statistics, Current Population Survey.

Source: BLS, Prestige Economics, LLC

PRESTIGE ECONOMICS   FI   THE FUTURIST INSTITUTE

Do you know why students are made to take classes they might hate? Because they might be spikes for some of those students. And even if they aren't spikes, they can foster metacognition.

Find Your Spikes at Work
Whether you find emerging spikes at school, or whether you bypass higher education and additional schooling after high school, you need to be on the lookout for spikes at work.

If you're like the average person, you will spend a significant portion of your life working. And this is an area where leadership potential is easy to recognize.

After all, how do you get promoted at work?

By being good at stuff.

You have experience and skills — and people build trust in you. But experience, skills, and trust take time to build. This is the importance of leveraging projection and support to more rapidly advance your career.

Of course, school and work are not the only places to look for spikes — to look for potential exceptional attributes.

Biology wasn't for me, but it might have been for someone else.

Find Your Spikes in Hobbies
Beyond school and work, there are often opportunities for spikes in areas where we have hobbies.

Since most people spend more of their time at work and in school than working on their hobbies, the odds of finding a spike in a hobby is less likely. But just choosing a hobby can indicate a potential spike.

A good friend of mine is a doctor who loves analyzing financial markets. He is inclined toward this professional field, and he has demonstrated a potential for success. But he plans on keeping his trading activities a hobby.

Some people want to keep their vocations — their jobs — separate from their hobbies and their avocations. But if you don't see potential for a spike — for an ability to excel in something academic or professional — then looking to your hobbies may offer insights into potentials.

Spikes and Time
It takes time to build spikes, and sometimes it takes a significant amount of time and effort to even identify potential spikes. For every Mozart or teenage doctor at Harvard, there are millions and millions of young people who have average development.

And that's all right. It's normal. Not everyone is special. *Special* by definition means "distinctive." This means that by definition we can't all be distinctive, unique, and special. We can't all be exceptional at everything.

But over time, people tend to show above-average abilities in some areas. And by nurturing these, you can build spikes.

There is a famous quote that speaks to this dynamic: "Everybody is a genius. But if you judge a fish by its ability to climb a tree, it will live its whole life believing that it is stupid." This quote is often attributed to Einstein, although that has been disputed.[2]

Nevertheless, there is truth in this quote.

Not everyone is good at everything or even the same things. But everyone has potential to excel at something — or many things.

To stand out, you have to be outstanding, but you don't have to be outstanding at everything. Ignoring things that are not spikes can be just as important as identifying things you are good at.

Furthermore, it is important to realize that some careers are average and may not require any spikes. But some careers have higher education and skill requirements. But it is also important to keep in mind that success is not measured by the same barometer in all careers. There are careers where remuneration is critical. Others where recognition is important. There are also others where personal impact and satisfaction are critical.

Whatever field you are looking to gain expertise in, you will still need spikes if you want to have exceptional success — however you define that, whether it be a financial outcome, recognition, or personal and social impact.

Spikes are by definition outstanding, and if you want to be outstanding, you need a solid foundation supporting you.

CHAPTER 7

PLAN YOUR SPIKES

In order to have spikes, you need to build on areas of potential excellence. And planning your spikes is an effective way to do that.

After you have found things of interest and potential, it can be quite valuable to plan how you will develop your spikes. This ties back into the concept of metacognition. Essentially, you are planning how to learn, how to grow your knowledge and network, how to scale your projection, and how to become an expert and leader with spikes.

But timing your spikes is important.

Especially in the early part of your career, building one spike at a time is critical. If you try to build a lot of spikes at once, it could slow down your career advancement and your move to significant perceived expertise.

But this path is not for everyone.

After all, some people prefer to be Renaissance men and women. But they risk being perceived as jacks-of-all-trades but masters of none — especially if they are perceived to lack focus in the early parts of their career.

Put simply: Choose the best and forget the rest.

- Am I great at X?
- Do I enjoy X?
- Could I be the best in the world at X?

You need to be hungry to succeed. But you also have to be deliberate in your planning.

Optimizing Levers
It is tough to find the dream situations, so try and optimize. There are, of course, four elements to build spikes: metacognition, experience, projection, and support.

But there are also three levers to build up those four elements: cost, time, and effort. Try to target the best ROI, with the lowest cost, shortest time, and least effort to build a spike.

Maybe you have more money than time, in which case you can push harder on the money lever. Or maybe you feel that you have all the time in the world, so you can invest more time in your spikes. Or maybe you can just really crank things out, and so your greatest strength is going to be the amount of effort you can provide in bursts to build and convey the expertise of a spike.

Whatever levers you decide to pull on more strongly to capture those four critical elements, it is important to always be asking yourself what you could be the best at.

If you can't think of anything, keep looking. And if you don't see it out there in the world, create something new.

As you plan the elements that support your spikes, also keep in mind that sometimes a great weakness can be the foundation of a great spike. Can you turn them to your advantage?

When I founded my economic and financial market research firm Prestige Economics 10 years ago, it was my intent to provide a high service to a small number of companies. We are not a multibillion-dollar organization, but we serve clients with combined market capitalization rates in excess of $1 trillion.

Our weakness is our relatively small size. But that is also our greatest strength. We are nimble. We can update our forecasts in a timely fashion. We have the freedom to write what we want. These are three strengths that our largest competitors do not have. And so we lever what we have.

As you consider committing to certain spikes. Consider where you have what economists call a comparative advantage. It is where you have strength that others do not have.

As one entrepreneur I know likes to say: There's riches in the niches. And this should prove true as you plan to build your spikes.

Scale Your Spikes

CHAPTER 8

COMMIT TO YOUR SPIKES

Once you have found your spikes, you need to commit to them. You need to focus on them — even if it means leaving other potential spikes behind.

The most important element of committing to your spikes is to view them as an investment. And as in all kinds of investments, it is best to start small before scaling up.

You don't want to overcommit early and fail.

You may need to start small and iterate before expanding and accelerating development. Some entrepreneurs and startup types refer to this as going slow and then going fast.

In short, it's important not to go all in on your very first poker game. You want to play a few hands before you make a potentially irreversible decision that could have significant consequences — either positive or negative.

This is actually a process I followed most closely when building up The Futurist Institute, which is a learning organization that I founded in October 2016. It was a move into future technology that started slowly but then accelerated more rapidly.

In 2016, I decided to expand my research and writing into the fields of new and emerging technologies. To foster this advancement, I completed a FinTech course at MIT in 2016. Concurrent to my coursework, I attended a conference that is held annually in Silicon Valley and that focuses on robotics and business. It is appropriately called RoboBusiness. At that conference, it became clear to me that a training organization was needed to prepare professionals outside the field of robotics for the coming imminent future of work, including automation, AI, and robots.

These two experiences were transformative, and I decided to build up a full curriculum of courses to train consultants, analysts, and executives to incorporate new and emerging technology risks and opportunities into their strategic planning.

Before building out our coursework, I wrote a book that was titled *Jobs for Robots: Between Robocalypse and Robotopia*. It was released in early 2017. It was well received, and it became a best-seller. With some further proof of concept, we recorded five core courses for The Futurist Institute. These courses were on the future of finance, data, energy, and transportation as well as futurist fundamentals.

By the end of 2017, I had released a second edition of *Jobs for Robots,* and I had created *The Robot and Automation Almanac*, with a collection of two dozen different essays on what to expect in the year ahead in robotics and automation.

Only in 2018 did we begin to have students taking our courses. We expanded our curriculum to nine courses from five. I launched a podcast called "The Financial Futurist," and I wrote a number of other books on new and emerging technologies. Now, we are negotiating multiple master service agreements with large private companies, public companies, and even governmental organizations.

And it all started with some courses and one conference.

As you think about how you will go slow and then go fast, consider the areas where you would like to project your experience — where you would like to be a recognized leader and expert.

Starting small might include reading some books and articles, or you may consider becoming an intern. A bigger step might be doing a certificate and a master's degree or writing a book on the subject.

A much bigger step is investing significant capital to create and scale a business. You want to be sure about the potential for a positive return before you get in too deep financially.

CHAPTER 9

BUILD, FEED, AND GROW YOUR SPIKES

A fundamental part of establishing your expertise is building your spikes. After you find, plan, and commit to your spikes, you need to lay a foundation to build expertise and feed your spikes. You have to make them grow.

As I discussed in the previous chapter, you don't have to be good at everything to start building your spikes, but you just have to be good at a couple of things — and potentially just one thing at first. And you need to focus on the four elements to build spikes in those areas.

As I've noted previously:

Spikes = f {Metacognition, Experience, Projection, Support}

Of course, there is one additional critical element of building spikes, and that's hunger. You need to want to have a spike. You need to want to be a leader. Because the process is not easy.

No matter how much you can growth-hack your way to leadership, there is still going to be a lot of work, a lot of strategic planning, and a lot of effort in building your platform as a thought leader.

Some personalities also lend themselves to building spikes. After all, you have to want to lead, and you have to be willing to pack in significant experience. You also have to be willing to project your expertise and be willing to build up a support network.

In the consulting world, people talk about individuals trying to build spikes. And the people who are most likely to push to get there are described as insecure overachievers.

But not everyone wants to work hard — or become a leader.

If you aren't willing to build up those four elements of spikes, then you may be dissatisfied with the pace of your career trajectory. Nothing good comes easy.

When I worked in banking, I spoke to a guy once who was ostensibly looking for a job. After finishing a degree, he was looking for a job. He wanted an introduction to a colleague who might hire him. He was a friend of the family, but I did not know him personally. Still, I was happy to make the introduction.

But when it came time for him to do a call with my colleagues, he sabotaged himself. He was unfocused. He talked about not wanting to work hard, and he talked enthusiastically about smoking marijuana.

To have that kind of conversation on any kind of professional call would be an embarrassment — let alone having that kind of call with someone who worked in an elite high-flying and high-paced role in an investment bank.

Fortunately, my colleague let me know what a disaster this guy was, so I wouldn't introduce him to anyone else. After all, someone with such little *savoir faire* also reflected poorly on me.

But his biggest problem wasn't that he portrayed himself as an avid drug user in an introductory phone call to an executive in an industry known for background checks and drug tests.

The truth is that these were merely symptoms of a bigger problem: He just wasn't hungry.

To this day, I doubt if he was ever able to build spikes. Or if he even wanted to in the first place. After all, someone who isn't hungry will struggle to develop a significant professional trajectory.

On the upside, someone who is hungry, who will work hard to put the key elements of spikes in place, will have more opportunities to build a career, to become a leader, and to become a respected thought leader.

CHAPTER 10

IGNORE FAKE SPIKES

One of the most valuable things you can learn in your academic or professional career is what you don't want to do.

I once had an undergraduate college counselor tell me that when you consider your future career and professional path, you are like a sculptor carving a masterpiece from a big block of stone. And for any sculptor, it is often just as important to know what you need to cut from the stone as it is to have a vision of what you want the final sculpture to look like. As such, knowing what you don't want to do can be just as important as knowing what you do want to do.

In general, it is important to make sure that you don't try to become an expert at something you don't like or are not good at. It could prove to be a significant waste of time — as well as a source of great frustration — if you try to gain experience in something where you are disinclined or lack natural abilities.

Just because you have to learn required material in school or you have to become proficient in certain tasks at work does not mean you have to build expertise in them. You don't need a spike in SAS just because you are required to use it. Of course, a spike wouldn't hurt.

The big takeaway I would share here is that if something does not seem to be a good fit, move on — at least for the moment. Of course, just because something does not seem to hold the potential to become a spike does not mean it won't be a potential spike later on. That's something I experienced in my own career.

When I was in high school, I struggled with calculus. In fact, I barely passed the course in my senior year. That struggle negatively impacted my perception of my math competencies significantly — and I shied away from math for years.

Given that experience in high school, I figured I would never use math again. I put it aside for a time, and I considered it would never be a spike. In fact, in my freshman year of college, I took the course Ideas in Math to fulfill my math requirement. The nickname for the course on campus was "Math for Morons."

Of course, I am a math guy now.

I live with numbers day in and day out, but it took almost seven years after high school before I would even attempt calculus again. I aced my calculus courses as prerequisites for my master's in applied economics.

While I worked on building up a spike in math, I could barely have fathomed one before. But after doing well in my courses, I started working on building the foundations to have a spike in statistics.

Finding the Way
There are a number of different tests that help people see their professional potential for spikes — and also to help them identify where they may not have spikes because they lack natural ability or because they are disinclined to work in a certain area.

This is the goal of the Myers-Briggs Type Indicator (MBTI), the Kirton Adaption-Innovation Inventory (KAI), and the Student Skills Inventory (SSI). These tests are designed to help uncover where people's natural abilities and inclinations are. It is also similar to the goal of The Futurist Institute's new Future of Work Personality Test, which is to help people know where their natural inclinations are.

In the end, it's important to not be distracted by fake spikes. Focus on those areas with potential. But don't forget to keep an eye on new potential spikes that may emerge.

Ignoring Your Fake Spikes
I would highly recommend taking the personality tests I have mentioned in this chapter as a way to help you identify potential spikes — as well as identify the fake spikes you should ignore.

CHAPTER 11

OUTSOURCE AND DELEGATE TO SPIKE

As with everything else in life and business, the more things that you can outsource and delegate, the easier it is to focus on your core activities and priorities.

This is also true when you want to build spikes, develop expertise, and demonstrate thought leadership. You may find that outsourcing and delegating will help you focus on your potential spikes.

If you can reduce the amount of mental real estate dedicated to tasks that feel like drudgery, you will increase the potential for having a greater impact on those areas where you want to project expertise.

This ties into a broader notion of avoiding doing things that you do not like. And it feeds into the theory of economic specialization. This is the theory that if people specialize, it increases overall economic output and potential.

Normally, the theory of economic specialization is something people talk about on a macroeconomic scale. For example, if country X can produce cheese more efficiently than country Y and if country Y is more efficient at producing wine than country X, then country X should just produce cheese and country Y should focus on producing wine. Because of the ability to trade, each of these countries benefits by focusing on what it does best.

While this is true for countries, it can also prove true for individuals.

I always try to focus on things that I enjoy and that I think I do relatively well. In fact, every year, I try to focus on things that I hate — and I make a concerted effort to stop doing them.

At the end of every year, I make a list of the things I like least about my job. And then I try to stop doing those things in the following year. I've done this for the past seven years, and it always makes me more efficient, more productive, and more effective.

It's a modified version of a process that some accountability and leadership groups call "stop, start, continue." In those kinds of exercises, companies focus on three things — they focus on the things they want to stop, the things they want to start, and the things they want to continue.

For me, the focus is on the "stop" pain points. And it's efficient. Honestly, it is always a good idea to delegate those things you aren't good at. Simply have other people help you.

There are people who can't write, so they dictate. Today, this can be done more easily and more cheaply than ever before. And why not? Almost every doctor in the 1980s had a Dictaphone. Even I dictated some things in the past. But I greatly prefer the writing process. I like having more direct and immediate control over the words I use.

Of course, there are people who can't do statistical analyses or calculations, so they use spreadsheets and computer programs. And why shouldn't they? This is why SAS and Excel exist.

Some people even hate giving speeches. And they delegate it.

While some people struggle with and hate these things, I *love* them. I enjoy writing and doing statistical calculations and giving speeches.

But I can't make a book cover or do artistic design to save my life. I make great charts and graphs. So, I have someone else doing our more advanced design work.

Leverage Others to Focus on Your Own Spikes
It's important to use the leverage of skilled subordinates and colleagues to focus on and build your spikes. If you can focus on what you do best, on where you excel, and on where you can have spikes, you can focus on your own thought leadership.

Fortunately, with companies like Upwork, finding skilled specialists is easier today than ever before.

Projecting Your Spikes

CHAPTER 12

SHOW YOUR SPIKES

Once you go through the process of building your spikes, you need to show your spikes. I cannot underscore enough the importance of sharing what you have learned, what you have researched, and what you have accomplished.

This is part of projecting your experience — both for external consumption and for internal corporate purposes — that I discussed in detail in Chapter 4.

The best way to show your spikes is if there are objective third parties that endorse your work and expertise. This could be any kind of ranking, like the forecasting awards we have been given by Bloomberg News. Or it could be a personal ranking, like the Forbes 30 Under 30 awards or any kind of other recognition. Another example would be the list of most influential financial advisors that Investopedia produces. That's a list on which I was happy to land last year.

Any of these kinds of objective lists provide validation.

Making sure you are being considered for these kinds of lists is important. If you are interested in one of them, it's a good idea to email the people who curate the lists and get details about the metrics and judgement around them. Then consider how you can take action to propel yourself into being considered for the list and ranking.

The kind of social proof provided by rankings and lists is similar to things like speaking at conferences, going on television, or writing a column for a publication. These are essentially third-party endorsements of what you are doing professionally — and they are good for showing off your spikes.

Opportunities to provide third-party validation of your work can be extremely valuable for projecting your expertise and building your path toward being a recognized thought leader.

In short, they are critical for building your spikes. And they can be invaluable for accelerating the timetable to demonstrating thought leadership.

CHAPTER 13

FAKE YOUR SPIKES

No one starts off as an expert.

You think Mozart's first notes on a violin didn't sound like a dying cat? You must be kidding.

Of course they did.

Every genius starts off as a baby, learning the same alphabet just like you and me. And they struggle at some things but become exceptional and great at others.

Everyone is a beginner at some point in their careers as well. The question is whether natural talent and hard work can cause a more rapid acceleration in development and can lead to a spike.

But in that time when you are developing whatever skills you may have to push yourself ahead, you are likely to go through something that almost everyone goes through as they push to be a recognized leader or thought leader.

You may need to fake your spikes — at least for a little while.

To put the challenges of expertise in context, everyone has their first report, first article, and first book.

Surprisingly, time goes by quite quickly, and if you set a plan to build your spikes in motion, chances are that you won't be faking it for very long. You may find that by following a pattern of best practices and repeated, planned, and learned behaviors, one day you will wake up and be an expert — without even noticing it.

Of course, everything is relative when it comes to building up your spikes — or even faking your spikes.

After all, in consulting, just one project can make you a legitimate expert in the eyes of your colleagues. But in other industries, claiming to be an expert after just one project would definitely be considered faking it. And you could be called out pretty hard for it.

On the flip side, what might be a scam to some people may seem completely legitimate to others. This is a big challenge when it comes to building the reputation you need to have as an expert and projecting your expertise.

Faking It: Drawback Number One
There are two big drawbacks when it comes to following the plan to fake it until you make it. On the one hand, it may be tough to know if you are going in the right direction.

I once had lunch with the head of the German office of McKinsey, and he bemoaned the fact that no one ever gave him any feedback. He was wildly successful by any stretch of the imagination. And yet he still wasn't sure if he was missing anything.

Since people are often loath to give feedback — especially upward feedback to a superior — it can be difficult to know how you are actually performing once you are viewed as a leader, an expert, and a thought leader with tremendous spikes. Once you advance, ironically, you may feel like you are faking it more because no one will give you feedback.

When it comes to projecting expertise, this can also be a problem because so seldom does anyone check your work. And unless you pay, it's tough to get real editorial feedback on content you produce. In effect, so many people are cranking out content and portraying themselves as experts that for many people out there in the world, it's tough to know what is real and legitimate. And this also makes it tough for aspiring thought leaders to know if what they are producing is valuable and insightful.

Faking It: Drawback Number Two
There is a second insidious issue related to the notion of faking it until you make it, and that is the risk of suffering from imposter syndrome. This is when you feel like you are an imposter. That you are not an expert. In fact, because everyone has to fake it until they make it, you may feel like you are still faking it long after you have actually "made it."

Even experienced professionals can often suffer from imposter syndrome, where they feel like they don't belong — like they don't have the spikes they actually have. In that case, you have to essentially continue to fake it even though you have made it.

This may sound a bit ridiculous, but it is a real challenge — and one that is part and parcel of a reality in which no one starts off as an expert and in which it is difficult to receive constructive criticism as people become experts.

CHAPTER 14

SPIKES IN THE AUTOMATION AGE

It's important to not waste your time on tasks where you do not have spikes. I discussed this in Chapter 11 with the importance of delegating tasks that do not contribute to your progress toward demonstrating thought leadership.

Beyond delegation, however, there is also another alternative method to gain leverage in your process to advance, and that's to outsource your spikes by using technology. In other words, you can use automation and technology to perform tasks that you find to be unpleasant and not constructive to becoming an expert. And you need to find as many ways as possible to do this.

Every dollar you spend on technology that automates a process you don't enjoy and that you do not need to be doing is a dollar that frees up your time. The ROI calculation on these kinds of expenses should be they value of your time freed up compared to the cost of the automated solution.

If the cost of automation is greater than the value of your time, then you may wish to hold off on automating.

But if the cost of automation is less than the value of your time, you should move forward.

And what is your time worth? That all depends on your billable hourly rate and your effective billable hourly rate.

To clarify: Your billable hourly rate is the amount of money you expect to earn for an hour's work. This might be your salary divided by the number of hours you work in a year. Or it might be the dollar-per-hour rate you offer for consulting services. Or it might be what you charge on Upwork for project-based work.

Your effective hourly rate, however, is different from your billable hourly rate because the effective rate is what you actually earn for your effort to get and perform the billable hours.

For example, if you get paid $100 per hour but it takes you three hours of preparation to secure one hour of work, you are actually working four hours. And that means that you are only earning an effective hourly rate of $25 per hour.

So, if your automated solution costs $50 per hour, it might look like a good deal compared to your $100 billable hourly rate. But it actually is not a good deal because it is twice as high as your effective hourly rate.

In sum, if your automated solution exceeds your effective hourly rate, it may cost more than your time is worth. But maybe it will still be worth it — especially if you are automating a task you do not enjoy or if it can somehow drive up your effective rate.

The Path to Curation

In growth hacking leadership, as in all professional activities, automation may not just free up your time, but it may be able to do things that you could not humanly plan to do, given actual human physical constraints.

Automated solutions can accelerate your path to leadership, but there is also a downside to using automation. And the downside is linked to how image cultivation and curation is driven online — by SEO values, beta-tested ads, and bots.

And none of that is going away.

This means that you have to be able to use these same tools to your advantage because people who can leverage technology to build spikes and their online presence as thought leaders will have more opportunities for advancement.

Essentially, automation gives rise to an accelerated form of content curation, leadership projection, and career cultivation.

Let me give you an example.

An Amazon bookstore — much like the Amazon shopping platform — is designed to be a highly curated experience. In one of the bookstores, all the books have top ratings.

This kind of phenomenon is going to also accelerate with expertise. As automation increases, we will see some experts become more visible than ever before due to curation.

Conversely, lesser names may fail to rise, or they may fade more quickly. This means you need to get spikey — and fast. This isn't to say that there are time-bound limits on projecting expertise, but it does mean that you will need to work hard to project expertise.

And one of the best ways to advance this process is to leverage technology to get there.

Your Spikes Automation
Use automation, chatbots, scripts, and the whole nine yards. This is especially valuable for repetitive tasks, like posting on social media or interacting online, sending emails, and other things that can be written into an automated script.

Finding the Right Support

CHAPTER 15

ENLIST SUPPORT TO BUILD SPIKES

How do you become a leader?

The answers are typically:
- Lots of time.
- Lots of experience.
- Lots of education.

As I've noted in previous chapters, you can cut the time part short by enlisting the support of others. This is why support is a critical element to becoming a leader and building spikes.

In Chapter 12, I discussed how endorsements and visibility help to provide support and social proof. But these aren't the only potential elements. Mentors are also critical as support who can help you as spike builders. But that is the subject of the next chapter.

In this chapter, I want to explore with you the importance of various kinds of professional support.

Consider the reality that people aren't born being great at anything — well, except at being a baby.

And they aren't very good at that.

A giraffe born in the African savannah can walk within 30 minutes.[1] It takes a human child more than 12 months. Clearly, you need others to survive from day one. But you also need people to grow and build spikes — and to ultimately achieve the greatest potential professional success, however you define it.

We are entirely reliant on others from the beginning. This is why one of the best things you can do to impact your life is to choose your parents wisely. It's a joke. But only sort of. In truth, your family can have a tremendous impact on your professional development. A great example of this is the fact that the statistically significant indicator as to whether you will become an entrepreneur is if your parents are entrepreneurs.[2]

Beyond childhood and throughout our lives, we rely on our family, our teachers, our coaches, and our colleagues to help us find support.

There is an often-cited literary notion about advancements where we are merely dwarfs standing on the shoulders of giants. The giants are those who came before us and those who support us now.

And the dwarf on the shoulders of those giants?

That's going to be you. So climb that giant!

Hopefully, by building spikes, you won't be just any dwarf perched up on high. You will be a dwarf with spikes.

And that will make you really stand out.

The main takeaway of this chapter should be that the aggregation of experiences of others can shorten the time it takes to become a recognized leader.

And I would further add that it is also my hope that the content of this book will allow you to consider me one of your spike builders.

I've got shoulders you can stand on too!

CHAPTER 16

FINDING THE RIGHT SPIKE MENTOR

I initially thought about titling this chapter "Finding the Right Spike Support." After all, support is one of the four key elements to building a spike. And there are many kinds of role models, mentors, and support systems you will come across in your professional career.

But the truth is that while there are different kinds of support that I discussed in the previous chapter, the most important kind of support that you explicitly need to seek out is from a mentor.

The storyline for many careers is sadly the same.

You scrimp. You save. And if you plan carefully and save diligently, and if you are lucky, then after many decades, just before you die, you may become a millionaire. But then, unfortunately, even if that happens, you pinch every penny because you know no more money is coming in.

And that's no fun!

You shouldn't have to wait that long to find financial freedom — to find success, to be a leader, and to be compensated accordingly.

You can get there more quickly, but you can't do it without other people. And keep in mind: They can be in different fields.

As one executive recruiter I know likes to say, you have to wait for someone to hand you the keys to the executive washroom.

The truth is that you can't get there without spikes. If you haven't been down a path, how do you know where it goes?

Positive Mentors
Ideally, you need positive mentors to succeed.

From a young age, we resist what others tell us.

Don't touch that. Don't eat that. Don't say that. Parents, teachers, peers. They all tell us what not to do.

But while people are quick to tell us not to do something, they seldom tell us what to do! And that's a big difference. The reason: When you tell someone "don't," their brain actually cuts out the "not." And this is generally true of negative statements.

Self-help gurus like Tony Roberts have written about the importance of positive thinking. And positive words. But this is also a core part of neurolinguistic programing theory, or NLP.[1]

We all only have just one life, but if we can aggregate the past lessons of others, this can be helpful in accelerating the process. Of course, not all advice fits in all cases. So providing a critical analysis of the advice you get is important.

There is a saying that was common at McKinsey when I was in consulting, that feedback is a gift! You have to accept it, but what you do with it is up to you!

But you won't get great at anything by someone saying:
- "Don't study that!"
- "Don't work there!"
- "Don't start a company like X!"

These are negative pieces of feedback, and they present problems.

Because our minds can't read negatives.

This means that positive messages are more important. We might interpret "don't" as "do" and "can't" as "can."[2] But if you want to grow, succeed, advance, and find financial independence, you need to focus on what you should, can, and must do. Rather than on the negatives that your mind may ignore anyway.

Plus, negatives tear you down while positives build you up. And positive feedback from a trusted source can help you build spikes.

This is what you want from a mentor.

The truth is that you need positive advice: Get to know X, study Y, get to know Z.

Maybe you know people who dole out this kind of advice.

It should be constructive and action oriented. A mentor that offers suggestions with an actionable outcome is likely to prove more effective than a mentor that always pushes you away from different potential ideas or strategies.

If they do it warmly, they might be a good mentor. Even if they don't do it warmly, and they are still sharing a positive message, that can be a big plus. And it can be indicative of a strong mentor. There is a big difference in messaging like "Don't study history" versus "Study accounting."

Accountability Groups
In the absence of an individual mentor, consider finding an accountability group; this is a group of people who are all working toward their own goals but who share progress with one another — and they hold each other accountable.

This is what groups like the Entrepreneurs' Organization (EO), the Young Presidents' Organization (YPO), and the World Presidents' Organization (WPO) do. They drive accountability for executives across different organizations.

To grow and to get spikey, you need strategies. And you need productive, positive advice — or accountability and positive encouragement.

One Final Thought

I would offer one final caveat about mentorship and accountability as it applies to peers in your field: It is important to not get caught up in the negative energy of other people's successes.

You are competing only against yourself. And if you keep this in mind, you are less likely to be distracted by the jealousy, envy, discouragement, or frustration that comes from comparing your successes to others.

Adapting Your Spikes

CHAPTER 17

SPIKES ON SPIKES

One of the big advantages of building spikes — of demonstrating thought leadership in one area — is that you can use this to build other spikes.

It's the first one that's the toughest.

When I founded The Futurist Institute, I was able to leverage the professional network, media contacts, and business experience I had gained by founding and building Prestige Economics eight years earlier. The spikes I had built in financial markets laid the groundwork for building spikes in the field of technology.

This means that I was able to leverage every success — and yes, every failure — of Prestige Economics to build The Futurist Institute and my spike in technology with less risk, at lower cost, and in a shorter time window than I had been able to build Prestige.

You will have the same opportunity to leverage your cumulative experiences as well once you have built your first spike.

After you have demonstrated that you are an expert, a leader, and a thought leader, you can use your experience, network, projection, and metacognition to build other spikes.

This is the notion of building spikes on spikes. It is the idea of letting your successes be the groundwork of your future endeavors.

Replicate Your Spikes
The biggest challenge as you explore new areas of expertise isn't being able to replicate spikes. It's about identifying what you want your next spike to be once you have been able to build up the first spike.

I discussed the metacognitive aspects of this process in Chapter 2. And the best way to move forward with a new spike is to codify, augment, and replicate the best practices that have worked. And to approach this process strategically.

But let's put it in more quantitative terms.

In his book *Outliers*, Malcom Gladwell famously noted that it takes 10,000 hours to become an expert on a subject.[1] If we assume this is right, what can we say about building a level of expertise that leverages previous experiences?

In other words, if you already have a spike to build your next level of expertise on, how many hours could you cut from that process?

What if you could cut the time to becoming an expert in another field — of having another spike — by 10 percent by leveraging your established expertise? I would argue that's a conservative reduction, and it would save you 1,000 hours, or roughly six months of work.

In reality, building a new spike on top of a spike you already have may drastically accelerate your timeline of projected expertise. In fact, by the thought-leadership platform you have already built, you may be able to reduce your time to be a recognized thought leader in a new area, with new spikes, by as much as 50 percent.

This makes building on your spikes a major way to hack your next level of success — a way to growth hack your way to the next run of leadership and thought leadership.

You just have to get to your first spike!

CHAPTER 18

RECYCLE YOUR SPIKES

One of the industries I do a lot of work with is the recycling industry. And there is a tremendous phrase in the recycling world that is quite apropos when it comes to growth hacking leadership, projecting, expertise, sharing content, and building spikes.

That phrase is "Reduce, reuse, recycle."

Reduce
In several of the preceding chapters, I have talked about using delegation and automation to reduce your workload. But it is also important to reduce the noise and distractions on your way to building a thought-leadership presence. And if you can, you should try and reduce your stress.

Working many hours or working with great intensity has a physical cost, so it's important to do everything you can to remain focused and not be distracted by things that can be eliminated with small amounts of money.

This could include everything from ordering premade meals to make for dinner as well as hiring a maid to clean your house. Maybe you hate these things, or maybe you love them. But if you don't have the proper time to allocate, even things you love can become a mental burden. Anything you can do to reduce your stress on those fronts frees you up to focus on your spikes.

When you travel, there can be a lot of stress as well. So you may want to order clothes, food, or other items to be delivered to hotels ahead of your arrival. One thing I regularly order to hotels is a clothing steamer. Normally, my clothes are wrinkled from being in a suitcase. And when I arrive at the hotel, I often don't have time for the hotel to press them. So, I just have my own steamer sent ahead. When I'm done with it, I either give it to housekeeping or I mail the steamer ahead to a future hotel.

Right now, there are three steamers out there in the world at hotels waiting for my arrival in the next eight weeks. This may sound like a strange way to "reduce," but those steamers reduce my stress. They cut down on the chaos. And that's the end goal. Find what reduces your chaos, workload, and stress — then do it!

Reuse

Aside from reducing your workload in areas that are not professional necessities, it might be a valuable exercise to focus on ways to reuse your content and reuse your skills in different areas and on different projects. In the previous chapter, I talked about building spikes on spikes, which is a way to reuse your ability to build your brand as a thought leader. But there are also more tangible things to reuse — like the written word.

You should be taking full advantage of reposting every part of a book you write on your own website, on a social media blog somewhere, and in smaller short posts on Twitter and LinkedIn.

After all, you are already doing the hard part. You are already creating valuable content. Now, you just need to squeeze the next level of marginal benefit out of it. And you can do that with the click of a button.

Recycle
The final strategy for content is recycling. This includes your ideas. If you have a good one, use it again and again. Find different permutations of what works, and recycle that idea. But you don't need to stop there.

You can also recycle other people's ideas, including expert ideas. Of course, you need people whose ideas you use. You aren't stealing someone's work. You are just recycling it. And providing credit doesn't hurt your argument. In fact, it can boost your ability to project expertise.

This dovetails with the notion I mentioned in Chapter 15 about dwarfs standing on the shoulders of giants. That's where you want to be — on top of other experts. Adding new things to a debate and dialogue that might also be able to draw in other experts to make new arguments and create new ideas.

And to project your own expertise — and create new spikes.

CHAPTER 19

CHANGE YOUR SPIKES

Sometimes your spikes just aren't enough.

That's when you might need to change your spikes.

In 2016, I realized that FinTech advancements presented potentially existential threats to my business Prestige Economics. And I knew that I had to find a way to stay ahead of a potential steamroller for my spike in financial market analysis.

Even though I was garnering quarterly top rankings for my accuracy from Bloomberg and I was frequently in the press, on the radio, and on television, I was worried it might not be enough if the disruption in FinTech was big enough.

Indeed, my concerns were not unwarranted. And so I began a process of changing my spikes. It was and has been a process not unlike that described in the previous two chapters, where I have tried to build spikes on spikes while also reusing and recycling some of my best strategies that got me there in the first place.

The spikes you may need to build in the future as a career pivot may be very different from your spikes now, but everything changes, and nothing is permanent.

On the upside, just because you are doing something now doesn't mean you have to follow the standard, tried-and-true pathway that has been worn so often before. This is just as true when seeking out new career opportunities or new fields of interest — or when starting a business.

Spikes can be augmented, but time is a critical ingredient for success.

Taking a very deliberate, strategic, metacognitive approach is the best way to hack the change and reduce your time exposure in the process. While some people prefer to gradually build spikes over time in a more organic way, this delay can be critical — especially if your company, career, or profession is on the edge of annihilation.

The most deliberate strategies to change your spikes are to plan early, test your aptitude for new spikes, build your new spikes, and invest in your new spikes. These are the same strategies you can use to build your first spike.

Hopefully, with experience, these phases will pass more quickly, and you will be able to hack the need to change — making yourself more responsive and more dynamic as well as less vulnerable.

If you have a vision for a new spike, you need to go for it. But you should still follow the same process outlined earlier in this book.

I realize that time may be of greater concern when you have to make a pivot, and this is why you should rely on your previous spikes as well as your metacognition, experience, projection, and support to help you move more quickly.

Regardless of how long building a new spike takes, you should have no regrets about your moves to build new spikes. After all, spreading your breadth as a thought leader is likely to bring with it a myriad of rewards.

One Warning
There are sometimes big trade-offs and steps backward if you want to change your spikes.

For example, experts get paid for speeches, writing, and consulting. They get promotions. And they can get other jobs. But very often, if you are trying to change your spikes, you may need to give away more of your work than you have in a long time.

After having been paid for speeches and articles, it may be painful to give away your writing, speeches, and consulting. But there is likely to be a direct correlation between how much you give away for free and how quickly you get things off the ground.

This means that if you want to still hold out to be paid all the time, it may delay the building of new spikes. After all, fewer people will be willing to pay for not-yet-fully-formed spikes.

CHAPTER 20

INVESTING IN SPIKES

The best investment you make in your entire life is not likely to be in financial markets, hard assets, or a get-rich-quick scheme.

The best investment you are likely to make is an investment in yourself.

While investing in a business venture you own may or may not pan out, an investment to build your spikes is transferrable whether you work for a public company, private firm, or yourself.

Furthermore, the best kind of investment you can make is a low-risk investment. And an investment in building your spikes is likely to present relatively low risks. It's not a leveraged financial contract in the futures market, where you can find yourself subject to a margin call.

Investing in your spikes is unlikely to result in a loss, and it can have a long-lived return. It is like an annuity that can pay dividends years — or even decades — into the future.

This is one of the reasons people pay ever-increasing amounts to attend universities — especially elite universities. After all, these contribute to spikes and can have a long-lived return.

We visited this data back in Chapter 6 and I have included it again in Figure 20-1.

As you can see, an individual in the United States with a high school diploma earns an average of $730 per week, while someone with a bachelor's degree earns an average of $1,198 per week.

That's a difference of $438 per week, and over the course of 45 years, assuming 50 weeks per year of work, the difference is more than $1 million in 2018 terms.

Figure 20-1: Wages and Unemployment by Education Level[1]

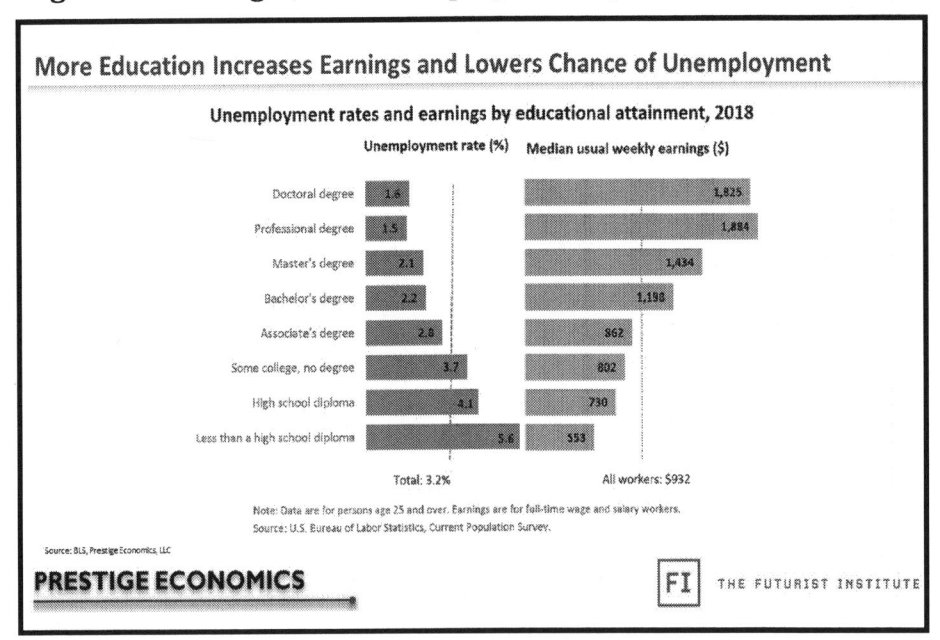

More Education Increases Earnings and Lowers Chance of Unemployment

Unemployment rates and earnings by educational attainment, 2018

Education Level	Unemployment rate (%)	Median usual weekly earnings ($)
Doctoral degree	1.6	1,825
Professional degree	1.5	1,884
Master's degree	2.1	1,434
Bachelor's degree	2.2	1,198
Associate's degree	2.8	862
Some college, no degree	3.7	802
High school diploma	4.1	730
Less than a high school diploma	5.6	553

Total: 3.2%   All workers: $932

Note: Data are for persons age 25 and over. Earnings are for full-time wage and salary workers.
Source: U.S. Bureau of Labor Statistics, Current Population Survey.

Source: BLS, Prestige Economics, LLC

PRESTIGE ECONOMICS   FI THE FUTURIST INSTITUTE

As you can see, there is a real dollarized ROI to pursuing education.

Of course, education really helps individuals the most by projecting metacognitive abilities and the potential for competency in the absence of significant — or any — experience. But education is only one potential element that projects potential and builds metacognition.

Informal education, certificates, and executive education also help project expertise and help you build spikes. These are also valuable investments that can help you build spikes and advance your progress toward leadership roles and your projection as a thought leader.

Building spikes is a good strategy for all professional occasions. It's true in boom years — and in bust years. During recessions, consultants often speak of a need to reinvent themselves due to the challenges presented by shifts in consulting opportunities.

In other words, while someone may be a thought leader in strategic growth, in a downturn that consultant may need to quickly retool to build up and project a spike in cost leadership.

No matter which spikes you build, if you become a thought leader, you will have countless ways to monetize that projection, including through career advancement, paid speaking engagements, ad hoc consulting work, and publications.

But building your own spikes is not enough.

Share Your Spikes

Beyond investing in and building your own spikes with delegation, automation, experience, education, and time, it is also important to share your spikes.

Spikes are ROI-positive endeavors that can require relatively small investments with low risk that have the potential to yield outsized returns.

And helping others build their spikes can benefit you as well.

While there is an altruistic reason to sharing your spikes and helping others, there can also be an unforeseen professional return from sharing your spikes, because it elevates your projection as a thought leader.

The more people you share your spikes with, the greater the reach of your impact and thought leadership.

CHAPTER 21

SPIKES AND THE ENTREPRENEUR

Spikes are different for entrepreneurs.

Unlike people in a corporation or trying to build a career by projecting spikes, entrepreneurs have their own maps. They are forced to build their own spikes. Entrepreneurs have to learn how to sell a better mousetrap to people who do not know they have mice.

Essentially, the challenges for entrepreneurs stem from a lack of platform and their inability to stand behind a big corporate name. Entrepreneurs do not have that ability to leverage a corporate brand to project their own personal brand.

As someone who worked for large corporations before starting my own firm, I can firmly recommend that one of the best things you can do to build your spikes is to take advantage of the corporate structure that exists in your organization. Use that support to its full potential because it will help you project your company's brand — as well as your own.

In other words, just working for a major corporation can provide some of the same validity as other third-party endorsements and validation. But if you strike out on your own, you will likely miss the support, the infrastructure, and the instant name recognition that comes with being in a big company. So, take advantage of it while you can!

The other thing that vanishes when you start your own company is a regular paycheck. For this reason, entrepreneurs are very driven by their need to generate income. They need to project their spikes even more effectively than other workers and companies because entrepreneurs keep what they kill. After all, entrepreneurs live and die by their own ability to generate income.

This means that while some people may be projecting spikes for a variety of reasons, for entrepreneurs it's about economics. It's about the money. This means that entrepreneurs are generally likely to be more directly focused on ROI compared to large companies with big budgets.

Of course, being an entrepreneur has major upsides as well. You get to build the job you want, and you have a lot of control over your time. And that is pretty great. If it wasn't great, I wouldn't be doing it!

Plus, no one will pay you what you're worth — except for yourself. And this also means that the financial rewards for being an entrepreneur are also potentially larger than for being a corporate worker.

The most important thing about becoming an entrepreneur is to choose your time carefully. Make sure your spikes are solid.

Consider this: The U.S. Internal Revenue Service (IRS) is not known for its generosity, and even the IRS lets a business lose money for three years before the business needs to demonstrate that it is actively trying to turn a profit.

In other words, your business is likely to lose money for several years before turning a profit. The time it takes to get a business off the ground is often called runway. And runway is a critical requirement for entrepreneurial success, which is why you need to make sure that your business can get off the ground.

You need to have sufficient funds to support the path to takeoff as well as potential clients that can support the business thereafter.

This is why it's important to build up your spikes and be prepared before you go out on your own.

So, just don't get fired and don't quit — at least not until you are ready!

Pulling Everything Together

CHAPTER 22

HACK YOUR SPIKES

Everyone I know is a hacker.

Everyone I work with and for. And everyone I associate with. They aren't hackers like Neo from *The Matrix*, but they are hackers who have found ways to crack a system. They have found a value arbitrage, they have become entrepreneurs, or they have found ways to advance within the corporate or professional structures in which they operate.

Just because you are doing something doesn't mean you have to follow the standard, tried-and-true pathway that has been worn so often before.

For me, the first system I hacked was financial markets. This deals with the relationship around how the Fed influences interest rates, which also influence the dollar, which in turn influence commodity prices — including oil prices. And these in turn influence the economy and inflation, which influences the Fed. I see this as a circular feedback loop.

When it comes to understanding the global economy, I see the economy as one big supply chain, with the U.S. and Eurozone economies at the most downstream parts, where we are the primary drivers of global demand in manufacturing and services. I also see China and India as midstream economies, and I see commodity-centric economies at the most upstream parts of the global economy.

These two frameworks, the circular market framework and the global supply chain framework, have helped me hack my understanding of financial markets and the global economy.

The Importance of Frameworks
Leaders hack. They develop frameworks to understand processes and relationships across entities, organizations, and individuals.

Even the concept of spikes that I have presented in this book has a theoretical and conceptual framework behind it:

Spikes = f {Metacognition, Experience, Projection, Support}

Now that is meta!

The frameworks that help you establish your spikes are likely to be different. But being an expert means translating complicated systems into easily digestible and discussable terms. And it means sharing these thoughts with others.

Your goal is to be a thought leader after all!

In short, helping others learn, understand, and be more effective is the most critical fundamental prerequisite driver that explains why leaders also get paid for what they know — and what they can share in a multiplicative fashion through content distillation and dissemination with others.

In reality, an effective leader is leverage for their entire team.

And a thought leader provides intellectual and conceptual leverage that extends well beyond their own firm — and potentially beyond their industry.

One core truth that I have tried to impart in this book is that your career will depend and be driven by your spikes and that your career trajectory will be directly correlated with the real and perceived spikes you build.

If you can make difficult concepts easy to understand through your writing and analysis, this will help accelerate your trajectory to thought leadership.

It is the greatest hack of all on your path to building spikes and becoming a leader!

CHAPTER 23

SHARE YOUR SPIKES

One of the most important things you can do once you have spikes is to share them. While people have mentored and helped you along the way, it is important to be a good mentor to others.

Once you get to a certain point in your career and professional development, you may find that there are fewer mentors around. This is especially true if you have managed to build spikes in critical areas. As your career changes and develops, there are people who have been down your path. And you need to find ways to connect with them.

If you cannot find mentors, you need to seek out an accountability group so that you have some form of encouragement and experience sharing that you can leverage to build your spikes to the next level.

By the same token, you also need to commit to helping others — to becoming a mentor.

Of course, if we revisit the notion from Chapter 16 that negatives tear down and positives build up, you need to recognize that it is important to provide positive feedback and support to people you mentor. Help the person visualize the outcome.

After all, positive feedback from a trusted source can help you build spikes. And that is the kind of mentor you want to be, right?

Teaching Begets Learning
There are also other benefits to being a mentor to others.

One of the big benefits at the top of the list is that it allows you to help share your experiences. In the previous chapter, I discussed the importance of creating frameworks and helping others understand difficult concepts in an easy-to-understand way.

By sharing with others — by teaching them — you also help yourself.

This ties into the National Training Laboratories' learning pyramid, which I have envisioned slightly differently in Figure 23-1.[1] In short, it shows that teaching others is the best way to retain information.

This means that by mentoring others and by teaching them, you can more firmly codify your own thoughts about the process of applying a metacognitive approach, gaining valuable experience, projecting expertise, or leveraging support. The more you can share about what you have done and learned, the clearer it will become to you.

This isn't to say you don't know what you're talking about. I mention this merely to highlight the importance of sharing as a way that you may unintentionally learn more in the process.

I know writing this book helped me codify my thoughts about spikes, metacognitive strategies, gaining meaningful experiences, projecting expertise, and finding support.

In fact, I have a checklist of to-dos that I will get to as soon as this book is off to the printer!

Building Your Support
Another benefit to mentoring others is that it can also help build your support network. Junior people don't remain junior for long. And they will remember your help or hindrance in the future.

Figure 23-1: Teaching Others Helps You Learn[2]

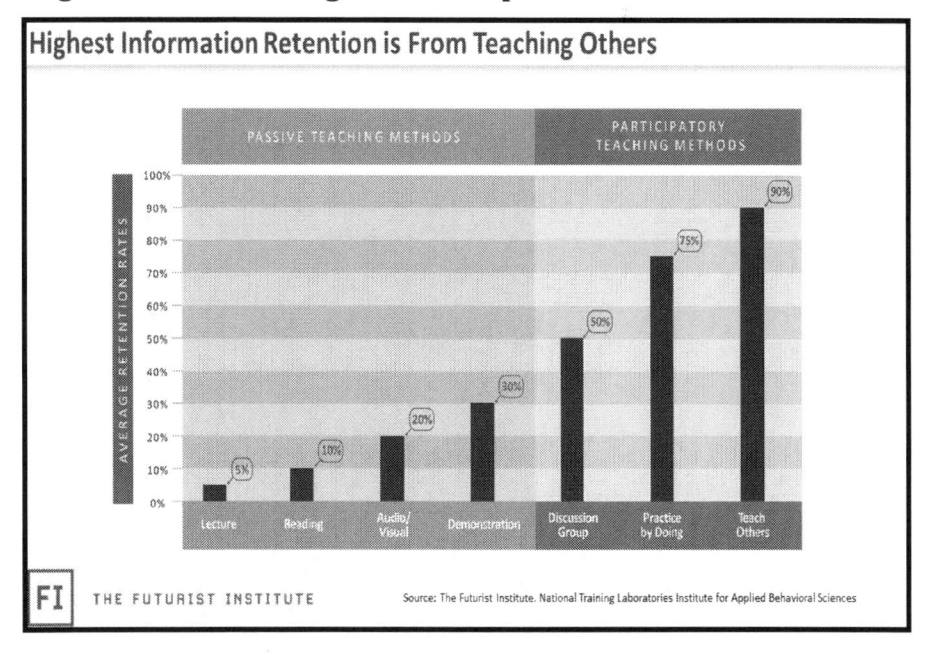

Highest Information Retention is From Teaching Others

Method	Retention Rate
Lecture (Passive)	5%
Reading (Passive)	10%
Audio/Visual (Passive)	20%
Demonstration (Passive)	30%
Discussion Group (Participatory)	50%
Practice by Doing (Participatory)	75%
Teach Others (Participatory)	90%

FI — THE FUTURIST INSTITUTE. Source: The Futurist Institute. National Training Laboratories Institute for Applied Behavioral Sciences

SPIKES: GROWTH HACKING LEADERSHIP 147

This isn't to say that you should become a mentor so that a mentee can help you in the future. But it might happen.

After all, major consulting firms all have training programs for junior staff even though the junior consultants and analysts may often stay for just a couple of years. But that support is something that those consultants are likely to remember long into the future — until one day they are executives and need to hire a consulting firm to support them.

Many firms have adopted this kind of strategy, where they "give to get" in a way that fills their sales pipelines for decades to come.

As an individual mentor, this shouldn't be your motivation. That would seem a bit cold and calculating.

But helping others can often provide surprising rewards for the mentor as well as the mentee.

CONCLUSION

SPIKES: GROWTH HACKING LEADERSHIP

My main goal in writing this book was to help you think about building expertise and becoming a leader by hacking a system of promotions and advancement that has long been dictated by time.

Hopefully, you now have some tools and strategies at your disposal that will help accelerate your timeline until you build your first spike — or one of many new spikes.

The benchmarks and trappings of success will vary greatly by individual, but the core elements that drive spikes and recognition as a leader and thought leadership are always the same: metacognition, experience, projection, and support.

If you can fill your professional satchel with those four elements, you will be on your way to building spikes — and maybe even spikes on spikes.

In essence, the four elements provide the foundation of leadership because leaders are required to continually demonstrate their ability to provide leverage to their people.

Leaders do this in the way they receive, digest, distill, and share information. In fact, these are the four critical roles of a futurist that I highlight in the Certified Futurist and Long-Term Analyst certification training program for The Futurist Institute.

There is endless content being generated out there in the world. And after reading this book, I expect that you will also be generating more thought-provoking content to project your expertise and build your spikes.

But that endless stream of content makes the ability to discern the worthwhile from the worthless an increasingly critical skill. And it will be critical in the future of leadership to not just create and share valuable information but to also cut through the noise of abundant content.

Further Learning
If you've enjoyed this book and want to learn more about the future of leadership and how to incorporate new and emerging technology risks and opportunities into your strategic planning, I would recommend pursuing the Futurist and Long-Term Analyst (FLTA) training program that I created for The Futurist Institute.

All of the details about the FLTA can be found at www.futuristinstitute.org.

Your Next Steps

There is a great Chinese proverb that the best time to plant a tree was 20 years ago but that the second-best time to plant it is today. Whatever your ambitions are, the sooner you plan out your pathway to thought leadership, the sooner it will become a reality.

This means that you have to be proactive and take steps today to move your career forward — to build your spikes now.

- Write that article today.
- Start working on a book.
- Sign up for a new course this week.

You can be the best — if you focus on your spikes.

But you also need to gain experience and project what you are working on. And if you don't share what you are thinking and what you are doing, no one will know.

On the one hand, it means if you don't know what you're doing and you don't share anything, no one will be the wiser.

But if you are serious about building spikes, if you are serious about being a leader — and being a thought leader — then you need to start sharing high-value content now.

Plant that tree of content, and let it grow into spikes.

You've got this!

ENDNOTES

Chapter 2
1. Retrieved on 18 April 2019 from https://www.activelylearn.com/post/metacognition.
2. Retrieved on 19 April 2019 from https://saylordotorg.github.io/text_leading-with-cultural-intelligence/s06-02-what-is-metacognition.html.
3. Retrieved on 18 April 2019 from https://www.activelylearn.com/post/metacognition.

Chapter 3
1. Retrieved on 19 April 2019 from https://www.inc.com/business-insider/elon-musk-says-you-need-to-work-80-hours-a-week-to-save-the-world.html.

Chapter 4
1. Retrieved on 19 April 2019 from https://www.bls.gov/news.release/pdf/tenure.pdf.

Chapter 6
1. Retrieved on 19 April 2019 from https://www.bls.gov/emp/chart-unemployment-earnings-education.htm.
2. Retrieved on 19 April 2019 from https://quoteinvestigator.com/2013/04/06/fish-climb/.

Chapter 15
1. Retrieved on 19 April 2019 from https://www.nationalgeographic.com/animals/2018/09/giraffe-baby-film-standing-birth-news/
2. Lindquist, M., Sol, J., and Praag, M. (April 2015). "Why Do Entrepreneurial Parents Have Entrepreneurial Children?" *Journal of Labor Economics.* Vol. 33, No. 2 (April 2015), pp. 269-296.

Chapter 16
1. Andreas, S., and Faulkner, C. (1994). *NLP: The New Technology of Achievement.* New York: Harper. Page 33.
2. Ibid.

Chapter 17
1. Gladwell, M. (2008). *Outliers.* New York: Little, Brown and Company.

Chapter 20
1. Retrieved on 19 April 2019 from https://www.bls.gov/emp/chart-unemployment-earnings-education.htm.

Chapter 23
1. National Training Laboratories. Retrieved on 19 April 2019 from https://www.educationcorner.com/the-learning-pyramid.html.
2. Ibid.

AUTHOR

ABOUT THE AUTHOR

Jason Schenker is the President of Prestige Economics and the world's top-ranked financial market futurist. Bloomberg News has ranked Mr. Schenker the #1 forecaster in the world in 25 categories since 2011, including for his forecasts of crude oil prices, natural gas prices, the euro, the pound, the Swiss franc, the Chinese RMB, gold prices, industrial metals prices, agricultural prices, U.S. non-farm payrolls, and U.S. home sales.

Mr. Schenker has written 14 books and edited two almanacs. Five of his books have been #1 Best Sellers on Amazon, including *Commodity Prices 101*, *Recession-Proof*, *Electing Recession*, *Quantum: Computing Nouveau*, and *Jobs for Robots*. He also edited the #1 Best Seller *The Robot and Automation Almanac — 2018* as well as the 2019 edition of the almanac. Mr. Schenker is also a columnist for *Bloomberg Opinion,* and he has appeared as a guest host on Bloomberg Television as well as a guest on CNBC and other television media. He is frequently quoted in the press, including *The Wall Street Journal*, *The New York Times*, and *The Financial Times.*

Prior to founding Prestige Economics, Mr. Schenker worked for McKinsey & Company as a Risk Specialist, where he directed trading and risk initiatives on six continents. Before joining McKinsey, Mr. Schenker worked for Wachovia as an Economist.

Mr. Schenker holds a Master's in Applied Economics from UNC Greensboro, a Master's in Negotiation from CSU Dominguez Hills, a Master's in German from UNC Chapel Hill, and a Bachelor's with distinction in History and German from The University of Virginia. He also holds a certificate in FinTech from MIT, an executive certificate in Supply Chain Management from MIT, a graduate certificate in Professional Development from UNC, a certificate in Negotiation from Harvard Law School, and a certificate in Cybersecurity from Carnegie Mellon University.

Mr. Schenker holds the professional designations ERP® (Energy Risk Professional), CMT® (Chartered Market Technician), CVA® (Certified Valuation Analyst), CFP® (Certified Financial Planner), and FLTA™ (Certified Futurist and Long-Term Analyst). Mr. Schenker is also an instructor for LinkedIn Learning. His courses include Financial Risk Management, Recession-Proof Strategies, Audit and Due Diligence, and a weekly Economic Indicator Series.

Mr. Schenker is a member of the Texas Business Leadership Council, the only CEO-based public policy research organization in Texas, with a limited membership of 100 CEOs and Presidents. He is also a 2018 Board of Director member of the Texas Lyceum, a non-partisan, nonprofit that fosters business and policy dialogue on important U.S. and Texas issues. He is also the VP of Technology for the Texas Lyceum Executive Committee.

Mr. Schenker is an active executive in FinTech. He has been a member of the Central Texas Angel Network and he advises multiple startups and nonprofits. He is also a member of the National Association of Corporate Directors as well as an NACD Board Governance Fellow.

In October 2016, Mr. Schenker founded The Futurist Institute to help consultants, strategists, and executives become futurists through an online and in-person training and certification program. Participants can earn the Certified Futurist and Long-Term Analyst™ — FLTA™ — designation.

Mr. Schenker was ranked one of the top 100 most influential financial advisors in the world by Investopedia in June 2018.

For more information about Jason Schenker:
www.jasonschenker.com

For more information about The Futurist Institute:
www.futuristinstitute.org

For more information about Prestige Economics:
www.prestigeeconomics.com

RANKINGS

TOP FORECASTER ACCURACY RANKINGS

Prestige Economics has been recognized as the most accurate independent commodity and financial market research firm in the world. As the only forecaster for Prestige Economics, Jason Schenker is very proud that Bloomberg News has ranked him a top forecaster in 43 different categories since 2011, including #1 in the world in 25 different forecast categories.

Mr. Schenker has been top ranked as a forecaster of economic indicators, energy prices, metals prices, agricultural prices, and foreign exchange rates.

ECONOMIC TOP RANKINGS
#1 Non-Farm Payroll Forecaster in the World
#1 New Home Sales Forecaster in the World
#2 U.S. Unemployment Rate Forecaster in the World
#3 Durable Goods Orders Forecaster in the World
#6 Consumer Confidence Forecaster in the World
#7 ISM Manufacturing Index Forecaster in the World
#7 U.S. Housing Start Forecaster in the World

ENERGY PRICE TOP RANKINGS

#1 WTI Crude Oil Price Forecaster in the World
#1 Brent Crude Oil Price Forecaster in the World
#1 Henry Hub Natural Gas Price Forecaster in the World

METALS PRICE TOP RANKINGS

#1 Gold Price Forecaster in the World
#1 Platinum Price Forecaster in the World
#1 Palladium Price Forecaster in the World
#1 Industrial Metals Price Forecaster in the World
#1 Copper Price Forecaster in the World
#1 Aluminum Price Forecaster in the World
#1 Nickel Price Forecaster in the World
#1 Tin Price Forecaster in the World
#1 Zinc Price Forecaster in the World
#2 Precious Metals Price Forecaster in the World
#2 Silver Price Forecaster in the World
#2 Lead Price Forecaster in the World
#2 Iron Ore Forecaster in the World

AGRICULTURAL PRICE TOP RANKINGS

#1 Coffee Price Forecaster in the World
#1 Cotton Price Forecaster in the World
#1 Sugar Price Forecaster in the World
#1 Soybean Price Forecaster in the World

FOREIGN EXCHANGE TOP RANKINGS

#1 Euro Forecaster in the World
#1 British Pound Forecaster in the World
#1 Swiss Franc Forecaster in the World
#1 Chinese RMB Forecaster in the World
#1 Russian Ruble Forecaster in the World
#1 Brazilian Real Forecaster in the World
#2 Turkish Lira Forecaster in the World
#3 Major Currency Forecaster in the World
#3 Canadian Dollar Forecaster in the World
#4 Japanese Yen Forecaster in the World
#5 Australian Dollar Forecaster in the World
#7 Mexican Peso Forecaster in the World
#1 EURCHF Forecaster in the World
#2 EURJPY Forecaster in the World
#2 EURGBP Forecaster in the World
#2 EURRUB Forecaster in the World

For more information about Prestige Economics:

www.prestigeeconomics.com

PUBLISHER
ABOUT THE PUBLISHER

Prestige Professional Publishing LLC was founded in 2011 to produce insightful and timely professional reference books. We are registered with the Library of Congress.

Published Titles

Be the Shredder, Not the Shred

Commodity Prices 101

Electing Recession

Financial Risk Management Fundamentals

Futureproof Supply Chain

A Gentle Introduction to Audit and Due Diligence

Jobs for Robots

Midterm Economics

The Fog of Data

The Promise of Blockchain

Quantum: Computing Nouveau

Robot-Proof Yourself

Spikes: Growth Hacking Leadership

The Robot and Automation Almanac — 2018

The Robot and Automation Almanac — 2019

Future Titles

Reading the Economic Tea Leaves

The Future of Energy

THE FOG OF DATA

The Fog of Data addresses the rising volume of data and describes the best ways to navigate data challenges — and how to derive valuable data insights. *The Fog of Data* was published by Prestige Professional Publishing in March 2019.

THE ROBOT AND AUTOMATION ALMANAC

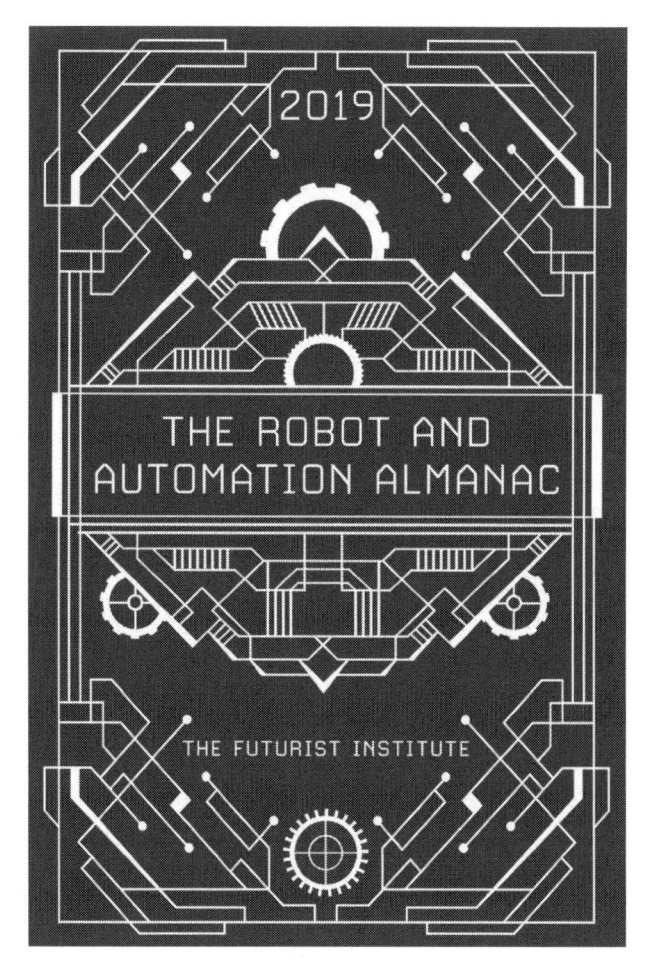

The Robot and Automation Almanac: 2019 is a collection of essays by robot and automation experts, executives, and investors on the big trends to watch for in automation, AI, and robotics in 2019. *The Robot and Automation Almanac: 2019* was compiled by The Futurist Institute and published by Prestige Professional Publishing in December 2018.

JOBS FOR ROBOTS

Jobs for Robots provides an in-depth look at the future of automation and robots, with a focus on the opportunities as well as the risks ahead. Job creation in coming years will be extremely strong for the kind of workers that do not require payroll taxes, health care, or vacation: robots. *Jobs for Robots* was published in February 2017. This book has been a #1 Best Seller on Amazon.

ROBOT-PROOF YOURSELF

Robot-Proof Yourself offers a number of practical professional recommendations for how to be robot-proof in the coming era of professional, economic, and financial disruptions. Robots and automation are set to advance, but individuals have a chance to benefit from the coming changes. *Robot-Proof Yourself* was released in December 2017.

DISCLAIMER

FROM THE AUTHOR

The following disclaimer applies to any content in this book:

This book is commentary intended for general information use only and is not investment advice. Jason Schenker does not make recommendations on any specific or general investments, investment types, asset classes, non-regulated markets, specific equities, bonds, or other investment vehicles. Jason Schenker does not guarantee the completeness or accuracy of analyses and statements in this book, nor does Jason Schenker assume any liability for any losses that may result from the reliance by any person or entity on this information. Opinions, forecasts, and information are subject to change without notice. This book does not represent a solicitation or offer of financial or advisory services or products; this book is only market commentary intended and written for general information use only. This book does not constitute investment advice. All links were correct and active at the time this book was published.

DISCLAIMER

FROM THE PUBLISHER

The following disclaimer applies to any content in this book:

This book is commentary intended for general information use only and is not investment advice. Prestige Professional Publishing LLC does not make recommendations on any specific or general investments, investment types, asset classes, non-regulated markets, specific equities, bonds, or other investment vehicles. Prestige Professional Publishing LLC does not guarantee the completeness or accuracy of analyses and statements in this book, nor does Prestige Professional Publishing LLC assume any liability for any losses that may result from the reliance by any person or entity on this information. Opinions, forecasts, and information are subject to change without notice. This book does not represent a solicitation or offer of financial or advisory services or products; this book is only market commentary intended and written for general information use only. This book does not constitute investment advice. All links were correct and active at the time this book was published.

Prestige Professional Publishing LLC

7101 Fig Vine Cove

Austin, Texas 78750

www.prestigeprofessionalpublishing.com

ISBN: 978-1-946197-07-8 *Paperback*
978-1-946197-06-1 *Ebook*

Made in the USA
Columbia, SC
30 April 2019